News about the von Boetticher Family

Courlandic Branch

News about the von Boetticher Family

Courlandic Branch

Reprint Of the 1. and 2. Books

NEWS ABOUT THE VON BOETTICHER FAMILY
COURLANDIC BRANCH

iUniverse books may be ordered through booksellers or by contacting:

iUniverse
1663 Liberty Drive
Bloomington, IN 47403
www.iuniverse.com
1-800-Authors (1-800-288-4677)

Because of the dynamic nature of the Internet, any web addresses or links contained in this book may have changed since publication and may no longer be valid. The views expressed in this work are solely those of the author and do not necessarily reflect the views of the publisher, and the publisher hereby disclaims any responsibility for them.

Any people depicted in stock imagery provided by Thinkstock are models, and such images are being used for illustrative purposes only.
Certain stock imagery © Thinkstock.

ISBN: 978-1-4917-9682-5 (sc)
ISBN: 978-1-4917-9683-2 (hc)
ISBN: 978-1-4917-9681-8 (e)

Library of Congress Control Number: 2016908004

Print information available on the last page.

iUniverse rev. date: 06/28/2016

Contents

About the Book

Friedrich Boetticher, second son of Carl and Emilie Boetticher, moved from Riga, the capital of Latvia, to Germany in March 1849. Here he bought a farm, got married, and then sold the estate and moved back Latvia with his wife in September 1853 to live in his parents' house during the winter months. Here his wife gave birth to their first child, Walter, in November 1853. In the spring, Friedrich moved back to Germany with his family to establish an art and book business.

When he was an adult, Walter von Boetticher, a medical doctor, came to visit his place of birth and to meet his relatives in Courland (a region in Latvia, also known as Kurland). Talking to his uncle Emil von Boetticher, he suggested that they research and write the first *News about the von Boetticher Family*. Walter wrote the first book about the history of the Courlandic branch of the von Boetticher family. Emil von Boetticher then wrote about his life and family with the help of numerous letters he had found that were written some 50 years earlier. This great work makes up the second book.

Both men did outstanding work for all the future generations of the von Boetticher family.

The original books were printed in Bautzen, Germany, in 1891–92. These were then reprinted in Hannover, Germany, in 2012. The books were translated between 2013 and 2015 from the original German text in the reprinted edition.

Jürgen von Boetticher, Translator

March 2015

Note to the Reader

The different dates of the month refer to the dates in the Russian and German calendars. The Russian date is 12 days earlier than the German date.

The given names of family members used from that point forward in the books are in bold. The numbers in parentheses after certain names correspond to the number of that person in the family tree.

For ease of translation, the endnotes, town register and name register were not included in the translation of the first book. As well, the endnotes, corrections, name register and town register were not included in the translation of the second book. From the reprinted edition, the appendixes of the family tree and map of Latvia were not included.

Because this is a translation from the original German text to English, this version includes changes with regard to differing conventions in the languages' written forms including punctuation and capitalization. The symbol † that is sometimes used indicates the date of a person's death.

Introduction to the Reprint

The first two books of *News about the von Boetticher Family* appeared in Bautzen in quick succession (1891 and 1892) and with the ambitious subtitle *First and Second Year*, under the editorship of the then genealogist of the family, Walter von Boetticher. A yearly print with following instalments was obviously planned at that time, but this was not possible.

In the first book, the focus was turned on a careful rejection of Zacharias, who, up to this time, was thought to be the progenitor of the family. The final focus went to the proven "Pastor phylogenetic tree," beginning with Nicolaus (1) and Christophorus (2). Attention was given to further general news about the family and a short report of individual life stories. The two life stories of the "progenitors," Carl Dietrich (11) and Johann Christoph (16), from the older and younger line were more detailed.

The second book, written by the youngest son, Emil (83), who served as mayor of Riga at the time, was devoted to the first councillor of the family in Riga, Carl Boetticher (38); his wife, Emilie; and their children. He writes in great detail about the lives of his parents. In many cases, he uses very personal letters and notes, which no longer survive. Business and private affairs appear side by side, and the trips into foreign countries, especially Germany, make up an important part of the book. It shows us the immediate family story and, more generally, the vivid life of an aristocratic-patrician family in Riga during the middle of the 19th century, in a form in which it rarely appears anywhere.

Due to the results of the wars of the 20th century, only a few copies of the two books have survived. Therefore, the family council decided to have these books reprinted. No alterations were made to the text or page structure. Added was an overall construction and a continuing page count through both books. In the appendix, there is now a map with the places that appear in these books marked, as long as they are in today's Latvia. Also, we find a family tree of all descendants and today's name bearers to make it easier to connect the names in the book to the individual persons to whom this edition is dedicated.

Manfred von Boetticher

August 2012

NEWS

about

the von Boetticher Family

Courlandic Branch

I. For the Year 1891

On Behalf of the Family Council

Edited by

Dr. Walter von Boetticher

Göda (Kingdom Saxony)

Manuscript printed in 100 copies

Bautzen
Printed by E. M. Monse
1891

Contents

Introduction

To the Members of the Family

The first (13) of November, the wedding day of Riga Councillor Heinrich **Carl** Johann and his wife, **Emilie** Constantie, née Wippert, is also the founding day of the Carl Boetticher family legat. The family council met regularly in Riga in the house of Mayor Emil von Boetticher and there, on November 1 (13), 1890, decided to spend the sum of 100 rubles of the legat for family historic news that would be of interest to the whole family and put it into print.

In his speech at the festive table, Mayor Emil von Boetticher reminded the members about the family's history since it had appeared in Courland and spoke of its future. His speech, the spirit and the idea of which is contained in the following pages, will be used as the introduction.

My dear guests! Again the first of November has brought a wide circle of dear relatives together for a happy reunion, and the effect of such uplifting reunion above the family life gives us the vision to look further about the daily time and place before us, so that our thoughts are able to go into distant pasts and the future before us and enables us to remember those who are no longer with us.

Looking back into the past, it is not necessary that I put everything that goes through my mind into words, but one question is appropriate: "What did the Boetticher family look like 200 years ago? Were there then, like now, also 27 family members together at a table? Had members of our tribe then already lived in this place, and had they found their domain here?"

Who is going to answer me this question?—So, nobody!—Have you never asked this question yourself, or is it irrelevant to you? Then I will try to answer this question, and we will see how far we get.

The year was 1690, when a highly respected man in Riga, the director of the high school since 1686 and professor working in jurisprudence and mathematics, Johann Paul Moeller, celebrated his wedding (his second marriage) with a patrician daughter, Margaretha Riegemann (now called Lövenstein). Among the many guests was also a pastor from Courland, who, as it was customary at that time, had composed his own poetry to celebrate this day. This pastor is our progenitor, the oldest proven of our origin. He had made the long trip from Blieden, where he worked as a pastor, to meet and celebrate with a friend from his youth. Here now they refreshed their memories, which they had brought along from the homeland. Moeller was born in 1648 in Erfurt. There his father once had a high position as a professor and regional mayor. His son had needed many years of study in different subjects to become a scholar. In the year 1673, he was a student in Erfurt, then in Wittenberg and Königsberg, and then 1681, he immigrated to Latvia and worked until 1686 as a house teacher. Our progenitor wrote a poem for him and signed it with "Nicolaus Boettiger, Pastor Blidensis." In it, he says how strange it is for a person to leave for a foreign country. The friend finds joy, luck and honour now on the shores of the Daugava River, "one wonders what could have been back home had we stayed there with Father's connection to the university and city hall, but the fatherland had taken a turn for the worst." Here we read that Nicolaus Boettiger came from Erfurt and knew the relationship between the town and the Moeller family and his connection to Riga's Professor Moeller, and this tells us that they, with all probability, were studying together in Erfurt. There a student by the name of Nicolaus Boettiger went to the university in 1663, so he was probably born sometime between 1643 and 1647, about the same time as Johann Paul Moeller.

There is no doubt that Nicolaus Boettiger is our progenitor, because in his letters, our progenitor Christophorus Boetticher speaks of his father being Nicolaus Boetticher, a pastor in Blieden. The orthography of the name at that time was not of great importance, so the difference in the spelling between the "ch" and the "g" gives us no doubt that the person is of the same identity, especially since a Boettiger and a Boetticher could not have been a preacher in Blieden at the same time.

It is not known if on his trip to Riga 200 years ago, Nicolaus took any of his family members along, but we believe he did not. On March 5, 1686, little Christoph was born and Nicolaus's wife, Emerentia Boetticher (née Preschkowin), did not want to make the arduous trip to Riga without the little child. And there was plenty of work at home in looking after her young son and teaching the older boy while their father was away. The older son was about ten years old at this time. We meet him later once more on August 18, 1712, in the parsonage of Nieder-Bartau, where he, at the baptism of the oldest daughter of his young brother Christoph, appears next to Mrs. Sophie Amalie von Behrin, Mrs. Korffin (the wife of a cavalry captain), and Mrs. Elisabeth Gravenstadtin (née Havenstein), as the godfather. His talent as a soldier got him into the army of Peter the Great, and he took part in the Nordic Wars. In these battles, which were decisive in the future of the Baltic provinces, he obviously showed luck and skill because in the year 1712, he became master billeting officer for His Majesty the Czar.

The soldier, Nicolaus Friedrich, as this Russian officer was later called, and the theologian Christophorus, so it appears, were the only children in the Blieden parsonage. They gave Mrs. Emerentia plenty of work, so there was no way for her to make the trip to Riga to celebrate. Now we find members of our family everywhere, but two hundred years ago, there were four people from our family living in Courland. At the wedding celebration, the representative of this tribe looked back into the past and found it strange that the fatherland "had lost its way" (referring to the Thirty Years' War) and immigration was necessary.

Should we not come to the same conclusion when we remember that seven generations have grown up here in this country since Nicolaus Boetticher immigrated and all have made an effort to build a new existence, so as not to stay in the old "ways"?

If we look into the future, do we see that we may not always be able to live here? Do any of you realize this?

How strange and wondrous is the Highest Hand that leads us, says Nicolaus Boetticher, 200 years ago, remembering the homeland, which he left because things had changed at that time. And now, where everything is supposed to change, the way our forefathers had planned and worked hundreds of years for our well-being—do some of you not feel a mighty pull back to the fatherland that Nicolaus Boetticher had left?

Will we still count 27 people in a few years on November 1 at such a meeting? This too is in the Highest Hand, but we are sure our family will be further pulled apart and therefore, it will be harder to keep a firm bond with all members and for everyone to keep a worthwhile memory from the past, which only some of you possess in the written form. Therefore, before we move apart, we must make an effort to collect all that will bring the scattered members intellectually closer together. We don't want to put these materials of a family history into a map, but we want to reach all the members and this can only happen in print.

The idea to establish a yearly family newspaper came from our brother Friedrich and nephew Walter. I thought of a different way and hope everybody will be happy and that includes the ones who came up with this idea. They may think that the conditions in the old home country are better than they really are. This will happen to the immigrants later. As the sun on our horizon sinks down, the rays, broken up by fog, reflect to us and always appear larger than the sun is in reality during the daytime. I believe there is not enough material for a family newspaper in a family as small as ours. But a printed record should be made of the past of our forefathers and all known family news that is important and of interest for all members—that is my thinking. This news will be kept for future generations, and no matter how far the family members are scattered, this will be a continuous connection between them so that the feeling of belonging never ends.

We who live together here, seeing each other often but only on November 1, still have the opportunity to talk and to get to know each other and relate to what is hidden in our written files—so we would not think of putting these materials into print. But the relatives living in faraway places have this wish, which has been adopted with sympathy at this meeting. They gave the impulse and pointed to the present, and they asked how many of the Boettichers will stay in the homeland of 200 years. So it is of importance to protect this 200-year history so it cannot be wiped out.

I just want to mention that the family council decided today, in case of the dissolving of the council, to put all costs toward the family foundation. Also the cost for printing documents and news that is important and of interest for the whole family will be paid by the foundation, and with this decision, I don't have to worry that I will have to pay for the cost of the printing.

Finally, I want you, the ones attending here, to think of all those who could not make it but whose thoughts were with us. They, too, met together for the same reason as we did. To our faraway living but still very close siblings and relatives with their wives and children, we say cheers! Cheers! Cheers! Cheers!

***

So our family news made its debut. Most of the contents come from the pen of Mayor Emil von Boetticher. Years of research did not lift the veil that hangs over persons and facts of the family before the middle of the 17th century. The immigration of Nicolaus from Germany into the new homeland, the poor documentation of the population at that time, the endless plagues with their terrible results for all citizens and especially the devastation brought on by the Thirty Years' War—these are the results that made it impossible up to now to get a certified, documented report of the family history of this time. Future research will bring us a final result.

W. H. Riehl says in his work *The Family* (Stuttgart and Augsburg, 1855) on page 261: "Every family should have the aristocratic pride, to point out the characteristic features. Therefore, she must collect and keep all documents that make this family special." To follow Riehl's reminder, here is the start with the first print. It wants to bring a true and complete record if possible; it wants to awaken memories of the past; and finally it wants to heighten the inner unity of the family members, even so far separated, and keep the connection alive for all.

With the interest that is expected of all the family members and with the active help by all, there should be no shortage of material for some more editions at certain intervals. Biographies of important family members, documents and letters important for the family, news about changes due to research in the family history, and copies of portraits of our forefathers, family estates, memorials, and more would be material for subsequent editions. May it be the wish that during the coming years, the *Family News* will develop into a house and family book, not only for the present generation, but also for the generations to come, and may they work further on it with love and express the sense as in the words of Goethe:

"Blessed be the ones who think of their fathers fondly!"

A.

Name and Coat of Arms of the Family, Legal Rights

The linguistic form *Boetticher* will be found just like the synonyms *Böttner, Büttner, Bädeker, Bödicker,* and *Bodmer* only in Middle Germany, as compared to *Boddenbender, Bender,* and *Binder* in the northwest and *Scheffler, Scheffner,* and *Schefmacher* in the southeastern parts of Germany. From an original subname, it became a solid family name; just like the overall language, so too did the family name change during the centuries in its orthography. In the sixteenth, seventeenth, and eighteenth centuries, when the written language was not yet common knowledge, we find the name for the same person as *Boetticher* or *Böttiger* and *Boettcher* or *Böttger*. In the Latinized period of the sixteenth and seventeenth centuries, besides the *Boetticherus*, we also meet *Vietor* and *Vannifex*. Since the time of Christophorus Boetticher (1686–1745), our family has written the name "Boetticher."

The von Boetticher family living in the Russian Empire and the Kingdom of Saxony uses the following coat of arms: on a blue shield with a green ground, a silver pelican with two young, a crowned open helmet, jewelry being wings in open flight, the right side blue and the left side silver. The covers are blue and silver.

As the family history of the 16ᵗʰ and 17ᵗʰ centuries has not been researched enough, we are not sure since when the family has used this coat of arms. It was not bestowed to them, but as we see these coat of arms variations used by many families, it was taken. If we ask the reason for these changes in the coat of arms, we assume that after Nicolaus Boetticher emigrated from Germany to Courland and became a pastor in Blieden, he stopped using his aristocratic title and changed his coat of arms to the way we see it today.

The allegorical meaning of the pelican and the young are known. The meaning is expressed in the church in Bischofswerda in Saxony with a distich beside a pelican picture.

Sanguine dat vitem pullis Aegyptius ales:
Tu mihi das vitam, sanguine, Christe, tuo.

It is known that our coat of arms especially is often found in Christian symbols. Already in the 14ᵗʰ century, we find the pelican on the seal of the religious clergy. Also the clergy of Zürich used it during the Middle Ages and clergy in the north had a coat of arms with the pelican on it. The remark by Hefner that the pelican (and the phoenix) is used as a "favourite picture on the coat of arms during the time of the wigs" and that they are "totally unheraldic animals" is rejected by Prince Hohenlohe; he gives may examples of the existence of the pelican in the heraldry in the 13th and 14th centuries and so proves that this is untrue.

It should be mentioned here that there is written proof that the museum's director in Berlin, Professor Carl Boetticher (born in Nordhausen, died in the year 1889), the old councillor of the Reich city Nordhausen, used the pelican and its young on the crown of the baldachin on the old Roland Memorial in front of the city hall, to express his hard work. Originally they were made from silver, but after the renovation of the Roland Memorial, it was replaced with a copper and golden coating, which is still there today. Nordhausen with the Dukedom Hohenstein is, so to speak, the cradle of many families with our name—presumably our family too originates from Nordhausen. Boetticher believes this memory of the father city is expressed here with the coat of arms of the family.

Our coat of arms does not resemble those used by many other families. It differs in its colours, and the pelican has two young ones on the shield, not three, as is often the case. Also, the pelican stands on green ground and not in the nest.

Commercial Councillor Carl Friedrich Boetticher, born in 1747, at his ennoblement in the year 1795, received the following coat of arms. The shield is split. In front is a standing anchor in gold; behind it is the silver pelican with two young in blue. Jewelry is the upright anchor. Up to the year 1795, he used the pelican with three young in the shield.

Let us talk about some variants of our coat of arms as we find it being used during the last century by some family members, as preserved with seal imprints. It is assumed that the reason for these changes and additions to the actual picture of the coat of arms was the aim to remember important happenings in their lives and to avoid the connection and relationship with another family of the same name. Was it legitimate to make these changes to the coat of arms, which was an inherited badge for the whole family and not just for the individual? This we will not debate here.

Colonel **Carl** Christoph Gottlieb von Boetticher, born 1772, shows a shield in the form of a cartridge with four parts: (a) two crossed sabers, the grip down, and above where they cross a cannonball; (b) a cross of the order; (c) three (2, 1) six-pointed stars; and (d) the pelican with three young. The jewelry is three ostrich feathers.

Later on, he changed his coat of arms as follows. The shield had four parts: (a) the pelican in the nest without young; (b) a green background without the shield; (c) a six-pointed star; and (d) an oak stump with two cutoff branches and two shooting leaves. The jewelry is three ostrich feathers. Both shields are surrounded by symbols of war—cannon barrels, sabers, and flags.

In the first variation, he points to his job as a soldier; in the second, he acknowledges his connection to the Braunschweig family with the same name by borrowing the oak stump from their coat of arms.

His brother, General **Gustav** Ernst, born 1788, used the same coat of arms as previously described with small changes in the sequence of the different fields. The shield rests on a medal star.

Mayor of Goldingen Johann **Friedrich** Boetticher (born 1749), the brother of the aforementioned **Carl** Friedrich Boetticher, had a split shield. Up front is the upright anchor, and behind is the pelican with three young. The helmet jewelry is two flames. As we saw, this same coat of arms was given to **Carl** Friedrich at his ennoblement, except the helmet ornament was different.

The coat of arms of **Johann** von Boetticher of Kuckschen (born 1793) has the pelican with three young in the nest. The jewelry was the open flight. Between them is a heart pierced by three arrows.

The high court lawyer Philipp von Boetticher (born 1777) used the same seal. Do the arrows indicate a relationship with the von Boetticher family in Nordhausen, whose coat of arms has two arrows?

The enclosed colour print of the coat of arms produced by an artist in the famous Heraldic Artistic Institute of C. A. Starke in Görlitz corresponds with all the demands of the heraldry. For a template, the artist used one of our similar coat of arms interpretations by Franz Behem in Mainz from the year 1550.

All members of the von Boetticher family, by reason of an edict from May 5, 1801, after an examination of the proof of nobility, as ordered by a deputation of the Lithuanian-Wilna government on August 21, 1820, were recognized as ancient nobility and registered in the nobility register of the Lithuanian-Wilna government. Following the resolution of the temporary session of the heraldic department of the ruling senate on September 29, 1842, and on September 6, 1844, the family was registered in the sixth part of the nobility family book of the Russian Empire. The coat of arms used by the family for a long time was endorsed on September 26, 1884.

By reason of an edict from a ruling senate on August 22, 1863 (No. 2330), all male descendants of the Councillor Heinrich **Carl** Johann von Boetticher, as long as they were subjects of the Russian Empire, were entered into the Courlandic family book for the immatriculated nobility not belonging to the Russian hereditary nobility.

Friedrich Heinrich von Boetticher, the founder of the Saxonian branch of the family, in Dresden, received the citizenship for himself and his descendants on November 3 (15), 1859, from the Kingdom of Saxony.

Rudolph Johann Heinrich von Boetticher, owner of Kuckschen, and his descendants in a direct line were, in the year 1882—according to a diploma from May 6, 1886—entered into the association of the Courlandic Knighthood.

Foundation of the Family

Heinrich **Carl** Johann von Boetticher founded the **Carl Boetticher Family Foundation** on November 1 (13), 1839. We will talk about this generous founder later on. From love for the family and for the care and welfare of it, "from the experience of the uncertain earthly luck and inspired by the wish to shield his descendants from innocent impoverishment in the future," on the day of his silver anniversary with his wife, Emilie Constantia (née Wippert), he made a contribution of 10,000 rubles for the family foundation. On December 31 (January 12), 1854, it had reached 21,000 rubles, and on November 1 (13), 1890, the capital had already reached the sum of 72,442 rubles and 29 kopecks.

Entitled to enjoy this foundation are:

1. the five sons of the founder and their wives and widows

2. all the married men of the descendants of the founder and their wives and widows, as long as the widows did not get remarried

3. all the unmarried female descendants of the sons of the founder up to their marriage

4. the three daughters of the founder and their husbands

5. the male descendants of the married daughters of the founder and their wives and widows as long as the widows do not get remarried

6. the female descendants of the married daughters of the founder, up to their marriage

The administration of the foundation according to the will of the founder was handled by four men of the commission, consisting of a member from the council, a clergy of the Evangelical-Lutheran city-church in Riga, a merchant of the trade, and a descendant of his family.

The statutes of the foundation were endorsed by the Riga council on August 26 (September 7), 1855 (sub. no. 7091), and had to be changed with regard to the dissolving of the Riga council in the year 1889. The changes were made by the council in the corroborations book for statutes on October 28 (November 9), 1889 (sub no. 8), in regard to the administration of the foundation. It now consisted of three members. They were:

1. one clergy of the Evangelical confession

2. one merchant

3. one family member living in Riga, who is in line to receive parts of the foundation as a descendant of the founder or

a husband of a female who is a descendant of the founder and who is eligible to receive parts of the fund

The administration has its seat in Riga. Should it be necessary to move the administration to a different town, it needs to be decided by two-thirds of the votes of the family council and the administration.

These words are for Heinrich **Carl** Johann von Boetticher, the founder of the family legat named after him, written by Goethe:

Es wirkt mit Macht der edle Mann
Jahrhunderte auf seines Gleichen:
Denn, was ein guter Mensch erreichen kann,
Ist nicht im engen Raum des Lebens zu errichen.

Drum lebt er auch nach seinem Tode fort,
Und is so wirksam, als er lebte:
Die gute That, das schöne Wort,
Es strebt unsterblich, wie er sterblich lebte.

A further foundation established by members of the family and administered by the family is the **von Boetticher Foundation**, existing with the Livlandic district committee as support account for the Evangelical-Lutheran churches. His joint heirs established this foundation after the death of the Riga councillor Heinrich **Carl**

Johann von Boetticher for the purpose of supporting the Lutheran county churches in Livland. One quarter of the yearly interest of capital is kept to enlarge it, and three quarters of the interest goes as one lump sum to a church or parsonage. The administration of the foundation is held by the Livlandic district committee under "support account," together with the members of the von Boetticher family, which has been designated by the administration of the Family Foundation of Carl Boetticher and the family council. This member of the von Boetticher family has to take part in all meetings, especially the one on November 1 (13) of every year to decide who gets the interest and has the right to vote.

The instruction of the foundation was confirmed on May 3 (15), 1878, by the central committee for support accounts for the Evangelical-Lutheran municipalities in Russia.

The capital of the foundation after the final count on November 1 (13) is more than 11,000 rubles.

Estates Owned by Family Members

Individual family members own the following knights' manors, estates and houses.

- in Riga: one large stone house on Georgen Street 1, owned by **Emil** Friedrich von Boetticher

- in the district of Witebsk: Dsernowitz, 3,200 hectares, owned by **Theodor** Philipp von Boetticher

- in the district of Wilna: Stephanpol, 2,800 hectares, owned by Mrs. **Anna** Elizabeth von Boetticher (née von Roques), widow of **Wilhelm Carl Friedrich** von Boetticher, who died September 10 (22), 1885

- in the district of Courland: Kuckschen, 2,375 hectares, owned by **Rudolph** Johann Heinrich von Boetticher

- in the district of Courland: Spirgen, 2,150 hectares, owned by **Theodor** Philipp von Boetticher

- in the district of Courland: Pommusch, 750 hectares, owned by **Gustav** Friedrich von Boetticher and his siblings

- in the district of Livland: Ebelshof, 185 hectares, owned by Carl **Oscar** von Boetticher

- in the district of Livland: Lievenhof, 110 hectares, owned by Carl **Oscar** von Boetticher

- in the district of Warshau: Dawidy (formerly an emperor church estate), 625 hectares, owned by the brothers **Victor** Carl Moritz von Boetticher and **Friedrich** Wilhelm Alexander von Boetticher

- in the Kingdom of Saxony: one country house, owned by Walter von Boetticher

B.

Genealogic and Biographic News

I. The First Accredited Documented Appearance of a Boetticher—The Boetticher Families in Erfurt, in Nordhausen, and in the dukedom Hohnstein in the Braunschweig region

Those von Boetticher family members residing in Courland and those repeatedly represented in Riga and in the Kingdom of Saxony originated in middle Germany. The Altmark seems to be the home of a number of families with our name. Werben, near the River Elbe, one of the oldest cities of the Altmark and a main stronghold against the pagan Wenden, is the place where we meet, for the first time, an accredited, documented Boetticher. On November 18, 1351, the margrave Ludwig von Brandenburg hands over the Wilden-Hof in Neuenkirchen to **Martin Bötcher** in Werben.

From the 15th century on, there are four main centers where we meet Boettichers: Erfurt, Nordhausen, the Dukedom of Hohnstein, and lastly Braunschweig. Beginning with Erfurt, we find a Boetticher family there in the early 15th century that had become wealthy. According to the residents' list, **Theodoricus Botiger** is the ancestor of the Erfurt branch. He immigrated as a rich man around the year 1400 into Erfurt and became a citizen there. His descendants are among the aristocratic patrician families, and we find the coat of arms when a Florian Boetticher became a councillor in the golden book of the council-transitus from the year 1655. During the 17th century, we find members of the family in Erfurt repeatedly as councillors, clergy and professors.

Nordhausen and the bordering dukedom of Hohnstein is the cradle of many Boetticher families. The proof of a connection between them and the families with the same name in Eurfurt—even though the distance between the cities is not great and their connection to each other is close—cannot be made up to this time. In Nordhausen, we meet a citizen, **Hermann Boetticher,** in the 16th century. He is mentioned in 1549 in a document as a witness among other "Citizens of Nordhausen." From his marriage to Elisabeth von Werther, **Peter Boetticher** was born. Peter was the chancellor of Duke Volkmer von Hohnstein and then appears as a chancellor in the diocese of Halberstadt under Duke Heinrich Julius von Braunschweig-Lüneburg in 1567. On October 24, 1563, the Roman king Maximilian II in Pressburg elevated him into the nobility of the empire. His many political activities cannot be mentioned here, but his strong commitment to the Reformation may have been the cause for Maximilian II, who was also involved with the Evangelical teaching, to promote him with this act of mercy. Duke Julius von Braunschweig-Lüneburg and King Maximilian II were friends, and so Peter had many benefits as a result of this friendship. He received a loan in the amount of 1,500 thaler from the Duke in September 1577. He also became the godfather of the youngest son of the councillor, Julius, on November 23, 1576, bringing a gift of three "Julius Lösern" (10 thaler). The councillor Peter gave a grant for students as a family scholarship, which is still in existence and is managed now by Pastor H. von Boetticher in Sprackensehl near Unterlüss (Hannover). The year of the death of the councillor is not known, but he must have died before 1583. His sons survived him: Jobst, Mayor of Nordhausen (died June 20, 1629); Burchard; Kanonikus von Eimbeck; Heinrich Ulrich, J.U.D.; and Julius. Jobst and Burchard seem to have kept the descendancy going, since the many documents about Peter and his descendants from the beginning of the 17th century in the royal state archive only talk about these two sons.

From this Nordhausen family comes **Carl Boetticher**, born in Nordhausen on May 17 (29), 1889. He was a well-known archaeologist and professor of the building academy in Berlin. His much younger widow went under the name Clarissa Lohde and was a well-known author.

From Nordhausen is the path to the origin of the family with the vice president of the Royal Prussian States Ministry, States Minister Dr. Heinrich von Boetticher in Berlin. This path becomes almost proof by the fact that his family had, for a long time, used the coat of arms given to the councillor. It has a blue and silver beam with a black greyhound wearing a red collar. Below the beam are two crossed silver arrows. It has an open helmet with a crown. The jewelry is the larger greyhound, and the sealings are blue and silver. The father of the minister, the chief president of the States Finance Ministry and privy councillor (died in Potsdam 1868), left three sons. The oldest son was privy finance minister and died in the year 1883 in Potsdam. The second was director at the Royal House Ministry and a senior civil servant and lived in Berlin. The youngest was a minister of state. In the year 1864, the family got their nobility statute back, and the previous coat of arms was changed so that the beam became a cross beam and the two crossed arrows under the beam showed an arrow above and below the beam in the shield.

In the area of Braunschweig, we meet many families with the name *Boetticher.*, The Braunschweig state secretary in Wolfenbüttel, **Zacharias** Boetticher, is named as a descendant of Chancellor Peter Boetticher. He was born in Gröningen in the Duchy Halberstadt on March 8, 1589, and died in Wolfenbüttel on September 1, 1646. This statement needs a correction, as a relationship between the Nordhausen family Boetticher and the Braunschweig family with the same name is possible, but there is no proof; the affiliation is not there. The parents of the aforementioned Zacharias were Zacharias

Boetticher, born in Groningen, principal of the school and then—since 1577—pastor in Groningen (died 1611), and Margarethe Stein.

Since some of the family researchers in our family point to **Zacharias** as a progenitor connected with the Braunschweig family, we need to check the descendants of Zacharias, and after that, everybody can make up his or her own mind and opinion.

State Secretary Zacharias Boetticher was married on October 25, 1631, in Wolfenbüttel, to the widow Ilse Papen, daughter of Controller Heinrich Schlicken in Minden and Agnes (née Reinecking), and had six children by this marriage. At the time of the death of his wife, who survived him by 20 years, there were three sons still living.

1. **Justus** Boetticher, born August 9, 1632, in Braunschweig and died March 12, 1712, in Wolfenbüttel, was a member of the Braunschweig privy council.

2. **Joann Heinrich** Boetticher, born October 24, 1638, in Braunschweig and died January 10, 1695, in Helmstedt, was a professor of law at first and later chancellor of the Prince Abby Quedlinburg.

3. The third son of Zacharias was not Johann Christoph, as de Lagarde writes, nor Zacharias, as some are saying, but **Julius Philipp**. According to the age of the second son, he must have been born between the year 1632 and

1638. He became a dean in Salzdahlum in the district of Wolfenbüttel and left one son, **Julius Gottfried**, who had no children. Dean Julius Philipp Boetticher died after he had been the dean for 33 years in Salzdahlum in April 1700 and was buried on the 25th of the same month.

The branch of Justus is doing well up to this day. The author of this latest news belongs to that branch, the branch of Johann Heinrich, whose descendant is the regional chairman and president of the Nobility Ladies Convent, J. G. von Boetticher, Ampleben (Braunschweig). He was born in the first half of this century, but his branch ended in the year 1869.

The Braunschweig family von Boetticher was elevated into the nobility of the Empire on March 3, 1717.

Since the end of the 17th century, the von Boetticher family has appeared in Courland and Semogiten and seems to be connected to a **Zacharias**, so we will mention all the ones with the name **Zacharias** from the 17th century that we have found so far.

II. Appearances of Personalities with the Name Boetticher in Livland, Courland and Lithuania in the 16th and 17th Centuries; The Courland Boetticher family—I Generation: Zacharias Boetticher, II Generation: Nicolaus Boetticher

Almost as early as in central Germany, we meet persons by the name of Boetticher in Livland, Courland, and the Duchy of Lithuania. Christoph Boddeker (also Boetticher) in the beginning was vice chancellor for General Hermann von Brüggeney, named Hasenkamp, then chancellor of the Master Order Heinrich von Galen, and his coadjutor Wilhelm Fürstenberg. On November 16, 1551, he was involved with the contract, where the Mark Duke von Brandenberg, Archbishop of the City of Riga, handed over the cathedral. Later on, he received the Estate Brucken from the master order, but was unable to make the payments and had to give it back to the widow of the previous owner. His son Johannes Boetticher (died 1637) was, since the beginning of the 16th century, a Riga councillor. A chronicle is credited to his name. It shows what happened in Riga and Livland during the year 1593. Soon after his death in 1637, we meet Nicolaus Boetticher (Klawes Boeddeker) in Riga. He becomes alderman in 1637 and in 1642 a councillor. He married Barbara von Ulenbruck. He died at 72 years old on January 14, 1658. There is no proof that the following councillors with the name Boetticher were relatives or that they and the people living in Courland and Lithuania with the same name were related.

In Courland, the family Boetticher appeared in the middle of the 16th century. Friedrich Boetticher became a Latvian preacher in Goldingen in the years between 1560 and 1565. He is the oldest known progenitor of the von Boetticher family in Courland and his grandson or great-great-grandson is supposed to be the pastor in Blieden, Nicolaus Boetticher (also Boettiger). All the known documents dispute the correctness of this fact, especially the one written by Nicolaus himself, as we will see further on.

Among the progenitors mentioned among the men of the family is also Zacharias Boetticher, but a lack of authentic material with information about his personality will mean a short review. Earlier on, the connection of descendency to Consistorial Secretary Zacharias Boetticher in Wolfenbüttel or other relative connections between the two was mentioned. With reservation, it is pointed out that the progenitor Zacharias and the aforementioned councillor in Nordhausen Zacharias Boetticher are believed to be direct descendants of Chancellor Peter von Boetticher with great probability. This Nordhausen Zacharias lived in the 17th century. All further news about him is missing at this time. It should be available as soon as the Nordhausen archives are in order and handed over for review, which hopefully will happen soon. Therefore, for now, we look at the oldest known progenitor of our family, **Nicolaus Boetticher**.

Nicolaus Boetticher (born?) died in Blieden between the years 1690 and 1700. He was a pastor in Blieden. The library in Riga keeps a poem written by him for the occasion of the wedding of Professor Johann Paul Moeller in Riga in the year 1690, which gives us proof that our Nicolaus was born in Germany. Yes! From these words, we conclude further that central Germany had been his home. Johann Paul Moeller, a son of Erfurt Professor and Governor Johann Moeller (died 1648), whose destiny had brought him to the shores of the River Düna, met there with the friend of his youth Nicolaus, when the disaster in his homeland had brought him to Courland, and used the occasion of his friend's wedding to wish him well with a sonnet. In it, he points to their lives together in Germany. "Our Fatherland," he calls the homeland of his friend and gives with his verses an accurate knowledge of their Erfurt background as only a child of the city or at least—in consideration of those times—someone who had lived in central Germany not too far from Erfurt could have made.

From family papers written by his grandchild, we also know that Nicolaus Boetticher was not born in Courland. In them, it says, "Nicolaus Boetticher, from Braunschweig-Lüneburg, where he had been a member of an aristocratic family, had come to Courland." The numerous difficulties for the Protestants in Germany during the

Thirty Years' War probably made Nicolaus Boetticher, like many other clergy, chose Courland as a place to immigrate, as at that time, it was protected by the trusted Duke Jacob (died 1682).

We don't know much about the life of our ancestor. On April 30, 1663, a "Nicolaus Boettiger" was registered at the University in Erfurt. No other information appears in the student register in the City Archive of Erfurt, and nothing is to be found about him. He was married to Emerentia Preschow. Neither in Erfurt, nor any other place in which we find people with our name during the 17th century, is there a name like hers. The names ending with "ow" show us with certainty that the family is of Slavic origin or at least went through the Slavonic countries. He passed away sometime between 1690 and 1700. His widow followed him in the beginning of the 18th century.

III.   Generation: Christophorus 1686–1745—Friedrich Nicolaus and Johann Christoph Boetticher

It is documented that Nicolaus had two sons: **Christophorus** and **Friedrich Nicolaus** and that all the Courland and Livland Boettichers are descendants of the first named. From this point on, the family news flows much more richly. One does not need to pick up occasional building stones to have material to build a family history.

Let us begin with **Christophorus**. The following is reported about him. He was born on March 3, 1686, in Blieden; enjoyed a good school in Courland; and because of the nearing unrest from war, attended school in Königsberg in Prussia in the year 1700. From this school, Löbenicht, he graduated in 1704 at 18 years old and started university in the same city. We find these words from him in the album of the Albertina: "October 4, 1704: Christophorus Boetticher, Blieda Curoky, Stip." The Thirty Years' War had brought brutality and a decline in the morale of the students and many professors of German universities. But it made room for serious studies of the arts and the new Pietismus regenerated the religious life and deepened the theological research. He received very little money from his mother but benefitted from a scholarship. Our Christophorus studied philosophy and theology for four years and listened to the then famous teachers in philosophy, Professors Rabe and Georg Thegen, M. Friedrich Stadtländer, and M. Gottfried Albrecht Pauli, and in theology D. Dentsch, D. Pesarovius, D. Walter, and especially D. Gottfried Wegner. In the year 1708, he defended a thesis under the guidance of Professor D. Gottfried Wegner, "De ambitu theologiae. Regiomonti 1708" (6 Bog. 40), and took a public exam at the Samland Consistorium. He was accepted afterwards as a candidate at the ministry. He had planned to be employed in Prussia, when Duke Friedrich Wilhelm of Courland (1692–1711) unexpectedly called him on September 25, 1710, to the preacher position in the Church of Ober and Niederbartau. "Here he found, because of the previous and still raging plague, everything in terrible condition; instead of two churches, only poor church spots." The newly appointed pastor held the service, depending on the weather, between the walls of the church or out in nature rather than in the big room of the office, in the hostel or in his parsonage, a miserable cabin ready to cave in. Only after the plague had passed did things slowly improve.

In the Boetticher family archive in Riga, Christophorus has left us some important dates in his life. He writes as follows:

On March 3, 1686, Sunday 4 o'clock in the morning, I, Christophorus Boetticher, P. T. Pastor Bartauensis, was born. My blessed father was Nicolaus Boetticher, Pastor in Blieden. My blessed mother Emerentia Preschkowin. On January 9, 1700, my blessed mother sent me to Königsberg to study. From there I was appointed by his high grace Friedrich Wilhelm, Duke of Liffland, Courland and Semgallen on September 25, 1710 as a preacher at the Church in Nieder and Oberbartau. Thereafter on February 4, 1711, I was examined and on February 5 ordained by Mr. Pastor Michael Rhoden in Libau and, on May 3, 1711, I was introduced by Mr. Pastor Rhoden. On June 29, 1711 I got engaged to the noble, respectable maiden Anna Hauenstein from Memel, who was born on May 9, 1692. Her blessed father was Mr. Thomas Hauenstein, Court Officer and also merchant in the royal city and fortress of Memel. Her blessed mother was Anna Catherina (née Zippelin). On July 30, 1711, I got married to the maiden Anna Hauenstein.

We now disregard the detailed reports of every child's baptism and the attending godfathers. Soon after the birth of the twelfth child, the marriage ended with the death of his wife. Here Christophorus reports: "My loved one gave birth to a premature stillborn son on February 21, 1728 at 9 o'clock in the morning and died peacefully on March 14 at 7:00 o'clock. May God bless her soul in the eternal life."

Christophorus did not want to remain a widower. In May 1731, he decided to enter a second marriage. City Governor Hespe from Heiligen-Aa and the forester from Rutzau were sent to Mr. Dienstmann, forester in Nieder-Bartau "to ask for the hand of his daughter." They brought back the "yes" to the sender on May 23. Then followed the engagement with attendance of the aforementioned gentleman on June 30, 1731, and the marriage took place with the maiden **Agnese Dienstmann** on September 6, 1731.

From this second marriage Christophorus had another four children. He did not have the joy to see all the children grow up.

His youngest child was only six years old when he "died softly and blessed to the Lord on September 17, 1745 at 3 o'clock."

"May God please keep his dear soul in happy eternity"—this last sentence is from an unknown writer to the own report of our progenitor.

He started in his position under the most difficult and depressing circumstances and worked steadily on rebuilding his parish as a reliable preacher, as we find proof hereof in the archive in Nieder-Bartau. Here, by his own hand, we see the register of the church members at the church services. Thirty-four years, he led his dear parish as a reliable Pastor until he retired in the year 1744. He only enjoyed one year of deserved rest.

In his activity as clergy, there is one more report of interest for us. At the dedication of the church in Heiligen-Aa in the year 1728, he gave a speech in the Latvian and German languages. But of special note, on August 28, 1735 (Dom. XII. p. Trinit.), he introduced Pastor **Johann Kühn**, the great-grandfather of **Ernst Kühn**, born June 18 (30), 1814, and died January 22 (February 3), 1856, in Rutzau and Heiligen-Aa. Ernst Kühn was married on April 30 (May 12), 1842, to **Caroline** Amalie von Boetticher.

There is an oil painting of our Christophorus with the inscription: "Christophorus Boetticher. Natus Ao. 1686 d. 3. Mart. Vocatus Pastor Bartaviensis d. 25. Septbr. 1710."

Nicolaus Friedrich, according to the opinion of Johann von Boetticher in Kuckschen, the youngest son of the pastor in Blieden, Nicolaus Boetticher, entered the Russian military service and so led a path that many family members took at the beginning of this century. Among the godfathers of his daughter Anna Catharina, born on August 11, 1712 (later the wife of Pastor Grundling in Kruthen), Christophorus also mentioned his brother **Nicolaus Friedrich**, who at that time was "quartermaster of his Majesty the Czar." If Nicolaus Friedrich was married or left any children, it is not known. But in general, we have no knowledge about his fate.

Johann Christoph von Boetticher, a major in the Grand Prince Lithuanian Army, was a contemporary and might also have been a brother but was definitely related to Christophorus and Nicolaus Friedrich. Through inheritance from his father, Zacharias, he got the Estates Jagelischki and Schimaize in Samogiten. He was married to Anna Latzki, daughter of the cupbearer Anton Latzki, from whom she inherited the Estate Girki. On July 15, 1703, Johann Christoph also received the Estate Kiwile as a lifelong beneficiary from King August II of Poland. Since September 8, 1729, his son, the Augustow owner **Christoph Boetticher**, owned the estates. He was married to Henriette von Mirbach. By the testamentary disposition, the Estates Jagelischki and Girki in the year 1751 went to the siblings

Carl Dietrich, born 1722, and Johann Christoph, born 1734, but were sold by the year 1770.

From the testamentary will, of which we have no knowledge regarding its contents, we can easily see the relative, a major in the Lithuanian Army, Johann Christoph, the son of Zacharias, and we also see our Carl Dietrich and Johann Christoph. A further conclusion that our family from Nicolaus (Bliedensis) on and the family of Johann Christoph (Zachariewitsch) had the same progenitor, with all the previously said, cannot be made.

IV. Generation: Children of Christophorus, especially Carl Dietrich (1722–1787) and Johannes Christophorus (1734–1807)

The Bartau pastor Christophorus had 12 children from his first marriage and four from his second. The following are their names and dates of birth and death as he had written them:

1. Anna Catharina, born August 11, 1712

2. Johannes Christophorus, born … 23, 1713; died January 23, 1727

3. Christina Elizabeth, born September 10, 1715

4. Friedrich Wilhelm, born October 26, 1716

5. Gottfried Andreas, born January 18, 1718

6. Alexandrine, born February 3, 1720

7. Anna Sophie, born June 12, 1721; died July 21, 1722

8. **Carl Dietrich**, born August 4, 1722

9. Anna Sophie, born March 7, 1724

10. Daniel Heinrich, born November 1, 1725; died December 8, 1725

11. Gottlieb Friedrich, born March 17, 1727

12. A stillborn son, born and died February 21, 1728

13. Marie Louise, born April 2, 1733

14. **Johannes Christophorus**, born December 26, 1734

15. Carl Friedrich, born February 5, 1737

16. Benigna Elisabeth, born December 4, 1739

Of these 16 children, four died during his lifetime (numbers 2, 7, 10, 12), and 12 survived him. Among the 12 children who survived their father, we focus especially on those who kept our family from extinction. These are the sons, **Carl Dietrich** and **Johannes Christophorus**, from whom the older and the younger branch have their origins. What we know about their life stories, we will thoroughly discuss later on. In the meantime, we will take our focus to the rest of the ten children and what is known about them.

Anna Catharina, born August 11, 1712, godchild of her uncle Nicolaus Friedrich, was married to Pastor Christian Gottlieb

Gundling in Kruthen, who had been a youth educator in her father's house in Bartau.

Christina Elizabeth, born September 10, 1715, married a doctor in Libau with the name Winziger.

Friedrich Wilhelm, born October 26, 1716, studied medicine. He lived and worked for a long time in Warschau. In his older years, he came back to Courland where he died in the year 1771, unmarried.

Gottfried Andreas, born January 18, 1718, studied theology in Rostock, where he was registered in 1735 as "Bartho-Curonus." Later on, he was a pastor in Preekuln and has to be mentioned as a cofounder of the Grobin clergy's widow and orphan bank. Only 34 years old and not married, he died in the year 1752.

Alexandrine, born February 3, 1720, became the wife of the merchant Kawen in Libau. Early widowed, she lived with her brother-in-law, the forester Reiss in Strehlen. She died in the same year (1771) as did her brother Friedrich Wilhelm.

Anna Sophie, born March 7, 1724, married the master forester in Strehlen, Johann Carl Friedrich Reiss, in 1746. He was born in Leipzig and was employed by Count Kettler, the owner of Essern. Mr. Reiss was greatly respected by Count Kettler and Duke Peter of Courland. Of his two daughters, we meet the younger, Anna Maria, who later married her cousin, Mayor of Goldingen Johann Friedrich

Boetticher (born 1749, died 1819), whereas the older daughter married Captain von Querfeldt, an estate owner in Lithuania.

Gottlieb Friedrich (Theophil), born March 17, 1727, became a doctor like his older brother Friedrich Wilhelm and probably emigrated to America.

Marie Louise, born April 2, 1733, the oldest daughter from the second marriage of Christophorus, married Doctor Becker in Libau. One of her sons entered the military and died as colonel and commandant (commander) of Minsk.

Carl Friedrich, born February 5, 1737, was only eight years old when his father died. It looks like later on he was still living in Nieder-Bartau. He may have been raised in the house of Pastor Christoph Ernst Kummerau, the successor of his father.

From Nieder-Bartau, on March 3, 1756, the following lines, which Carl Friedrich wrote into the family album of his brother Johann Christoph are dated:

"Wer auf der Erde lebt und nicht nach Thaten strebt,
Die Sterbliche vergöttern können;
Der Lebt in einer Nacht, die Niemand sichtbar macht,
Und mag sich selbst der Tugend Glanz nicht gönnen.

With these lines I send greetings to the owner of this book, from his true brother C.F. Boetticher."

We also know that Carl Friedrich had academic training and married a Miss von Haudring. He reached an old age and spent the last years of his life in the city of Birsen.

Benigna Elisabeth, born December 4, 1739, the youngest daughter of Christophorus, married Pastor Kerkowius in Birsgalln. She died without children.

***

Our special interests are the two progenitors **Carl Dietrich** and **Johann Christoph**.

Carl Dietrich Boetticher (August 4, 1722 to September 26 (October 8), 1787), was born on August 4, 1722, in Nieder-Bartau and on the sixth day after his birth "by the bond of mercy of the great God received the holy baptism." A doctor of theology, Wilhelm Willer of Memel, a Pastor Dietrich Stavenhegen from Durben, and a theology student, Dietrich Bernewus (?) were the godfathers at the baptism. The devout father, who wrote the names into the baptism register, added these words: "The holy ghost give him (the baptized) growth and increase his age, wisdom and grace by God and the people. Amen."

Carl Dietrich received his first schooling from the highly educated Christian Gottlieb Gundling, his future brother-in-law, who was a house teacher up to the year 1735 for Christophorus Boetticher and then was called to the preacher position in Kruthen. In the same year, the next oldest brother, Gottlieb Andreas, left his parents' house to study theology in Rostock. Carl Dietrich was 13 years old at that time, whereas his next following brother Gottlieb Friedrich was only eight. We don't know if a new teacher was employed for them or if this was impossible with the meager conditions in the parsonage. The preparations to get Carl Dietrich into a career as a scholar were given up. Instead, he started his apprenticeship with a merchant Schulz in Libau. In this small but busy merchant town, he found new fields of interests. After his apprentice time, he left Libau. We know that a Prince Radzivil employed him as a private secretary.

In the year 1746, at 24 years old, he moved to Goldingen as a merchant on July 27. In the same year, he was sworn in as a citizen and got married to the daughter of the owner, von Warduppen, Dorothea Goetecke.

At that time, among the cities of Courland, Goldingen held a superior position. The city government was "built upon the Wendisch and Wolmar Laws," special laws protecting the free vote of the towns' council, and trade and business were in the hands of well-organized citizens. Up to this time, the Jews played no role in the cities of

Courland. The dukes of Courland who had resided in the old city on the River Windau had always tried to improve the cities of the dukedom but especially "Goldingen had to be admitted." Old laws had to be defended in Goldingen, and new ones had to be made. In order to establish them, men with insight and power were needed. Carl Dietrich Boetticher had both qualities, and his fellow citizens soon recognized this. Already in the year 1755, he was voted in as city councillor, and on October 22, 1755, he gave his "oath as a Goldingen City Councillor." From then on, Carl Dietrich worked with all the strength and duty he could in his new position. He was a man who concentrated on the goals ahead with a clear vision. We get a sense of this smart businessman by looking into the business ledgers he wrote, which reveal the author as being a cunning man of the law. It was no wonder that Carl Dietrich was appointed to the highest position when that position became vacant.

> On September 15, 1761, so it says in the Goldingen document ledger, Mr. Councillor Carl Dietrich Boetticher, was, praevia abdicatione Dni. Consulis Tobias Kolzsch, who had been the Mayor for seven years and eight months and had left to the City of Grobin, voted to be Mayor and head of this City of Goldingen, sworn in and confirmed, also hoc facto put on the Mayor's Chair and seat from the Alderman in the name of the

city and at today's citizen convention in our City Hall cum gratulatione vice versa facta, entered and signed.

Deus ter optimus maximus, qui hanc electionem sua duxerit sapientia, huic Domino Cousuli, munere hocce spectabili dignissimo, suo assistere velit auilio et grafia divino in omnibus ejus actionibus et inceptis. Illum que bona et constant beare sanitate, vires corporis et animi largiri benignissime, Omnia singulaque negotia sua coelesti coronare benedictione, sempiternam concordiam, tranquillitatem et pacem condonare ac quaevis ad bonum et optatum perducere scopum.

The great enthusiasm heaped on Carl Friedrich Boetticher and the called for blessings sure brought good results. He was mayor for 26 years; he led with "much fame and honour," so that his "name and remembrance by the city and all now living and future citizens will not be forgotten and kept with honour."

One of the main character traits of Carl Dietrich was incredible perseverance with anything he undertook that for him seemed right and good. He was the perfect man "Justus et tenax propositi" when it came to defending the City of Goldingen in their deserving patronage rights and to protecting it against the appointment of city civil servants. Here he used his strong personality for what he knew was right. In Hennig's *Story of the City of Goldingen*, we read on page 270:

> When the congregation met on September 15, 1766 to vote for a new candidate (preacher), a dispute arose between the congregation and the city government, were last mentioned strongly objected pointing to their jus compatronatus. A few times the election was unsuccessful. It ended in a lively court case that was known up into Poland and went on for 15 years. The reigning Mayor Boetticher was the soul of it all. It had cost the city quite a bit of money but they were awarded with the jus compatronatus in 1781.

It is also known that Carl Dietrich had sacrificed his fortune in this court case for the welfare of the city. "I hope," so he writes in an instruction to a lawyer to make a written complaint, "in a successful passing, because I am convinced that our case is a just one and our sovereign is gracious and wants to see his cities and their leadership grow and prosper."

The Mayor of Goldingen counted on goodwill of the duke when it was of importance for the city, and the duke knew that Mayor Carl Dietrich was of a special class. Duke Peter had said once to his people that he only had one mayor in all of Courland. As someone tried to correct him and pointed out that every city had a mayor, the

Duke replied: "I only have one smart Mayor in Courland and he is Boetticher in Goldingen; he would be good for a larger city."

A silver service with the inscription "Donum a duce serenissimo Petro Consuli Goldingensi Boetticher. Anno 1770 d. 17 Aug." is still owned today by the descendants of the former mayor of Goldingen and is a valuable reminder of their friendly connection to the duke. A part of the silver service had to be given to the French as a contribution in the year 1812.

Carl Dietrich Boetticher ended his active life on September 26 (8 October), 1787. He is the founder of the older branch of the Boetticher family. As was customary at that time, he had written the names of his relatives on the last page of his hymnbook, which was entitled: *The Repentant Payer of His Duty.* It also showed the dates of birth and baptism and all the godfathers.

His four children were:

1. **Carl** Friedrich, born June 29, 1747

2. Johann **Friedrich**, born June 25, 1749

3. Susanna Gottlieb, born November 21, 1750

4. Marie Louise, born April 24, 1753

***

Johannes Christophorus Boetticher (born December 26, 1734; died December 14 (26) 1807), or **Johann** Christoph Boetticher, is the progenitor of the younger Boetticher branch. Of the birth of his oldest son from his second marriage, **Johannes** Christophorus, the pastor in Bartau tells us: "On December 26, 1734 mornings at 10 o'clock my dearest gave birth to a young son, who was baptized on January 1, 1735 by Mr. Pastor Tyddaeus from Libau and given the name Johannes Christophorus." Then followed the names of 13 godfathers, mostly guests from Libau, and at the end these words: "The Holy Ghost may let him grow up to honour his name and to the delight of the parents. Amen."

Johann Christoph was only 11 years old when his father died in 1745, and things changed drastically in the parsonage in Nieder-Bartau. How long the widow of Christophorus stayed afterwards in the parsonage is not known. In July 1746, Christoph Ernst Kummerau was introduced as preacher in Ober- and Nieder-Bartau: At this time, the widow of his previous colleague probably left the place where her husband had worked for a long time. She married for the second time to Pastor Ernst Friedrich Wagenseil, who was ordained on August 27, 1754, in Birsen. Two years earlier, her oldest son, Johann Christoph, went to the university in Königsberg where he was registered on October 6, 1752, and there studied law until the year 1754. At that time, 21 men from Courland with whom Johann

Christoph was closely associated studied in Königsberg. These friendships lasted right into the later years, and Johann Christoph outlived all his Courlandic University buddies. After Judge von Gohr died in 1805, he was the only one left from his circle of friends of the Königsberg times.

After moving back to Courland, he became town secretary in Goldingen. His stepbrother Carl Dietrich was, at that time, a member of the council, and that may have been the reason why he moved there. A short time later, Johann Christoph switched from his first job to take the position as secretary at the Tuckum District Court. He stayed here as instanz secretary until he died in the year 1807. In the following year, his son **Friedrich** Wilhelm Heinrich was the appointed successor.

He was married to Katharina **Elizabeth** von Kurowska, named Hennisch (died November 25 (7 December), 1821), and the happy couple had many children. Only ten of the 24 children reached a ripe old age. Much appreciated for his business sense and his hard work, Johann Christoph was the centre of attention in the wide circle of the small Tuckum. Many hikes into the neighborhood and a yearly stay at the beach resort Ploehn broke up the daily grind in the office. The relationship of the family with other people was kept with old Courlandic hospitality and affability in a friendly way, whereas in the close family circle love for each other ruled in a relaxed atmosphere.

We read about it in a letter written to the Supreme Court lawyer Phillip Boetticher (born 1775; died 1829) as follows:

> It is great if the love among the siblings is not interrupted by distance, but the opposite is the case. Our family gives here a very good example and if someone talks about unity and warmth, we are always mentioned. May God keep us this conviction, which is a beautiful monument that our dear parents, who set an example of love and unity gave to us.

To typify the honourable head of the family, we quote here part of a letter written by him. When his son, **Friedrich** Wilhelm Heinrich left for the university in Jena in 1793, he wrote, among others, the following words in his family album:

> Nobody should count on a steady blissful happiness, who has not chosen the correct means—and these are: the right reverence of the highest nature, the drive to live virtuously, and to try to become a useful member of society; the three points contain the advice for a noble appropriate life ... With your education that you have received and the fundamental principles that you know, I am certain you will reach all these goals ... My son, I love you so much and I am proud of you and that you will be an example for the younger generation

in the search to become noble. My dear son, this great hope I set in you, and you will not disappoint me …

These few lines show us the characters of both the father and son and the nice relationship they had. The personality of the mother, Mrs. Katharina **Elisabeth** von Kurowska, shines through in a letter to her son in the year 1815. She wrote to her "dearly loved Guschin" (Gustav Ernst Boetticher, born 1782; died 1847), who had just gotten a promotion to colonel:

I know for a long time already that you are a crafty devil and you will always be one. Where are the promises: "Old Manning, I will write to you as soon as I get home." Now the old Manning can wait until she turns black, waiting for mail—but it's all right; I know you are a good person and you love me. Write soon and all will be forgotten! … My dear Moritz [**Moritz** Johann Ernst Boetticher, born 1777; died April 3 (15), 1848] always writes, I know, no matter where he is,—but you rascal, you promise, but you don't keep your word. Still, even so, you will always be my dearly loved Guschin and you know it well. The Kleisten sends greetings to you: Last night we visited there. It was Knapcheese on the table; and she said these cheeses are made for the colonel. Now we have to eat them ourselves. A few days ago I talked with Mrs. Sacken from Lipsthusen. With tears in her eyes she thought of you and thanks you for the greetings that you had sent to her. "Who could have known that our dear Gustav becomes a colonel when we talked with each other so kindly in Gaiken …" The old Miss Sacken had previously lived in Tuckum but now lives in Schwarren, is totally blind now and very sick. She had held you for your baptism. She and I thanked God, tears of joy running from her blind eyes, "that her Gustav had become so successful!" If Baron Rönne from Puhren who was also your Godfather, would still be alive, I am sure he would have been happy like a father for you and say: "Wai mon nau Labaroka; tas schelmis bie gruti turret, kas winam as par augstem letam pe Kokla Karrajas!"—All your siblings kiss you dearly through me. The small Fahsel (the grandchildren) thinks often of you but not Oscar. He is thick and fat. Goodbye, may God bless you! …

Johann Christoph died at 73 years old on December 14, (26), 1807. His wife lived during the time she was widowed with her son Friedrich Wilhelm Heinrich in Tuckum. Here she lived highly honoured and loved among the children and grandchildren and by all who knew her. When she got older and was unable to visit the near estates as she had in her earlier years, the friends who lived there came to see her and had good fun in the company together. She was deeply religious, and she made sure that her children and grandchildren found their way to the loving God. Every morning, she held a prayer with them.

On the one hand, she went through great pain seeing more than half of her 24 children die at an early age. Also her son Georg, only 22 years old, a lieutenant, was killed in 1810 during the capture of Basardschik. On the other hand, she lived to see her surviving sons succeed in their professions and the recognition they received. Two of them were jurists; three others served in the army and as officers were steadily promoted. The decorations they received held the old mother in a constant transport of delight. Philipp, one of her sons, writes: "her religiousness and trust in God was beautifully rewarded here, as heavens have so obviously protected the brothers (in the wars) and they have to thank in part their religious mother, who had prayed for them."

She outlived her husband by 14 years and died on November 25 (December 7), 1821, in Tukum.

On a hill near Tuckum, at a spot where she and her family had spent many happy hours enjoying the view of Courland's fertile fields and the surrounding hills near the forest, is her grave where she is buried next to her dear husband.

Life-size portraits of the couple painted in oil are in the possession of Privy Councillor **Alexander** Friedrich Johann von Boetticher in Riga.

Here are the names of the ten children from this Tukum branch that reached a ripe old age:

1. **Friedrich** Wilhelm Heinrich, born 17___(?); died 1831

2. **Carl** Christoph Gottlieb, born 1772; died 18___(?)

3. **Philipp** Gustav, born 1775; died 1829

4. **Moritz** Johann Ernst, born 1777; died 1848

5. **Gustav** Ernst, born 1782; died 1847/48

6. Georg

7. Elisabeth

8. Johanna

9. Caroline

10. Constanze

V. Generation

    A. The children of Carl Dietrich, especially

       (1) **Carl** Friedrich (1747–1815)

       (2) Johann **Friedrich** (1749–1819)

B.   The children of Johannes Christophorus, especially

(1) **Friedrich** Wilhelm Heinrich (177__–1831)

(2) **Carl** Christoph Gottlieb (1772–18__)

(3) **Philipp** Gustav (1775–1829)

(4) **Moritz** Johann Ernst (1777–1848)

(5) **Gustav** Ernst (1788–1847/48)

A.   (1) **Carl** Friedrich Boetticher (born in Goldingen June 29, 1747; died in Mitau June 15 (27), 1815), the oldest son of the mayor in Goldingen, **Carl** Dietrich Boetticher, was a merchant. The conditions in the small city of Goldingen were not to his liking, so he moved to Mitau, where he built a large circle of activities. His hard work and many different activities soon made his business very successful, and he became quite wealthy. He purchased, among other things, the Estate Plahnen in Courland, which was still owned by the family later on. Many honours were bestowed upon him. In October 1776, the king of Poland, Stanislaus August (1732–1798), awarded him with the title of Commercial Councillor, and on November 12 (24), 1795, he received from Franz II, the last Roman-German Kaiser, in a ceremony, a Diplom that honoured the aristocratic status of his family.

Carl Friedrich was very industrious. He not only tried to improve his own wealth; he constantly looked to help his fellow man, which he liked more than ownership and honours. Carl was not married but was very much involved with the education of the children of his younger brother Johann **Friedrich**, who after the War of 1812, had lost his fortune. All his wealth was given to the children of his brother, who died a short time after him. He died in Mitau on June 15 (27), 1815. His thankful surviving dependents honoured him with this poem:

Das Hochgefühl, nicht Dir allein zuleben,

Nein—mehr für Andrer Wohl bemüht zu sein,

Das war Dein Stolz! Dein eifriges Bestreben

Auch ungesehn die Armen zu er freu'n.

Drum wirktest rastlos Du im Sein hinieden,

Stets unermüdet, bis an's Lebensziel,

Und fandest so in Dir den sel'gen Frieden,

Dass Deiner Tat es Dankes Zähr entfiel.

An impressive memorial at the cemetery in Mitau stands on the spot where Carl Friedrich, after a busy life, found his resting place. The memorial was put up in thankful memory by the sons of his brother, and the administration of the von Boetticher family legat looks after the maintenance.

A. (2) Johann **Friedrich** Boetticher (born in Goldingen June 25 (7 July), 1749; died in Riga May 10 (22), 1819. The younger son of Goldinger Mayor Carl Dietrich, just like his older brother **Carl** Friedrich, became a merchant. He stayed in Goldingen and offered his service to the father city by entering the Citizen Guard where he was elected to cavalry captain. This followed the appointment from the king of Poland, Stanislaus August, to an officer's rank. On October 10, 1776, he married a cousin, Anna Maria Reiss, the daughter of the Oberförster (chief forester) in Strehlen, Johann Carl Friedrich Reiss, and Anna Sophia (née Botticher). Five years later, he joined the city government, where he, like his father, moved up to the highest positions. We read about it in the Goldingen document book:

On September 26 (October 8), 1781, Mr. Johann Friedrich Boetticher, citizen and merchant and also Cavalry Captain of the green guard, was voted (per plurima vota E.E. and W.W.) as Councillor into the City Council. On September 7 (19), 1787, the honourable, respectable and wise Mr. Councillor Johann Friedrich Boetticher in publica convocation per plurima vota was voted to Court Steward and confirmed. On September

15 (27), 1790 Mr. Court Steward Johann Friedrich Boetticher in publica convocation did his officium praetorianum, and after a new vote, he again was per plurima vota voted to the position of Court Steward and confirmed.

After the introduction of the city administration law for the cities of Courland, Johann Friedrich became representative of Goldingen. The Russians introduced these laws. After the old laws of city government under Kaiser Paul, he became mayor. During the many years of change, the activities for the City of Goldingen— the downfall of the Polish Republic, the Dukedom of Courland, the annexation into the Russian Empire, the reforms of the empress Katharina II and then immediately following the introduction of the old order by Kaiser Paul—were all carried out. It was a highly charged time politically. To represent the City of Goldingen at that time was a real challenge. Worse than the experience of the last century was the bad time of the war year 1812 for Johann Friedrich in which he had heavy financial losses. Tired from the pressures of that year, he went into retirement. The last years of his life, he spent in Riga with his oldest son. Here he enjoyed his time with his dear wife.

Johann Friedrich did not possess the guts or the toughness of his father in the way he pursued his goals. He was of a mild and peace-loving manner, polite with everyone and always there to help if it was in his power. So his wife had to help out. She was an energetic woman with a keen mind; she was also polite and courteous. This was the result of a good upbringing whereas the mild manner of her husband came from his heart. The couple was always very polite with each other. When they went to the dinner table, Anna Maria offered to let her husband lead the way, and only after he had bowed to her politely and given her the honour, would she walk ahead. He followed his dear wife, because she was ruler of the house.

Johann **Friedrich** died in Riga on May 10 (22), 1819, in his 70th year of his life and his 44th year of marriage.

What he had previously established in his occupation was put into the obituary written by Mayor F. M. Berg (the father of future Riga Councillor Berg). It says:

> He will not be forgotten and lives forth in the hearts of the citizen of Goldingen who had given his best for our city, the late Mayor Boetticher … Not only did he dry the tears of the needy during his life but looked to make improvements for the future generations. Before he died in Riga, he made a gift in conjunction with his heirs for the poor in Goldingen in the amount of 200 ruble with the interest paid yearly on the day of his passing into a better world for the people in the Goldingen poorhouse.

A few years after Johann Friedrich, his widow died on _____, 18____.

During their many years of marriage, they had 11 children. Here are their names and birthdays:

1. Carl Friedrich Gustav, born August 5 (17), 1777

2. Friedrich Gottlieb, born August 9 (21), 1778

3. Susanna Marie Caroline, born February 28 (March 12), 1780

4. **Carl** Heinrich Johann, born March 5 (17), 1782

5. Gottlieb Sophie Anna Friederike, born February 7 (19), 1784

6. Wilhelm Christoph Leopold, born February 6 (17), 1784

7. Hieronymus Gotthard, born April 4 (16), 1788

8. Constance Caroline Anna, born September 23 (October 5), 1790

9. **Johann** Christoph Ernst, born February 20 (March 4), 1793

10. **Gustav** Dietrich, born December 25 (January 6), 1795

11. Friederike **Amalie** Sophie, born July 14 (26), 1801

Of these 11 children, only the sons **Carl** Heinrich Johann (4), **Johann** Christoph (9), **Gustav** Dietrich (10), and the daughter Friederike **Amalie** Sophie reached a ripe old age.

B.   (1) **Friedrich** Wilhelm Heinrich von Boetticher (born in Tuckum

_____, 17____, died in Tuckum _____ July 1831)

As we just saw, the father and son of our Boetticher family were mayors in Goldingen. In Tuckum, the oldest son, **Friedrich** Wilhelm Heinrich, followed his father, the court official **Johann** Christoph Boetticher, who had died in the year 1807, into the position that his father left. Therefore, Tuckum stayed at the centre for the widely distributed siblings of the court official Friedrich Boetticher. Also, their elderly mother, Mrs. Katharina **Elisabeth** (née von Kurowska), lived in his house in her old age, right to her end. **Friedrich** Wilhelm Heinrich, called by his parents and siblings "Fritz," was born in Tuckum on _____, 17____. He grew up in the close-knit family and went with the well wishes of parents and friends in the year 1793 to the University in Jena, where he was registered on September 29 (October 11) of the same year. The old university on the River Saale, at that time, was where Reinhold, Fichte and Schiller taught; it was the city where the teachings of Kant had found its followers and had great magnetism for the sons of Courland. They tried not to be influenced by the world's happenings and enjoyed the life of a student. It was the time of the Sturm und Drang period, not only in literature; the time of the "awakening of reason" was also mentioned in the family book. A real Courlander did not get involved in these kinds of reflections. The good advice was "Your homeland is the whole world," and he rejected all influences and was strongly pulled back to his God's country. Fritz, too, came back to Courland in the year 1795, where he shortly thereafter started as actuarial at the Kandau Court. By an order of the Courland government, on January 29 (February 10), 1808 (Sub No. 134), he was confirmed in the position of secretary at the Tuckum Court (court official), and he worked there until the year 1825. He died in Tuckum in July ____, 1831.

On _____, 18___, he got married in Tuckum to **Agnese** Anna Pusin, born in Tuckum on December 6 (18), 1785, a daughter of the Tuckum pastor and later Probst in Kandau, Carl Ernst Pusin, who after a happy but short marriage, outlived her husband by 25 years and died far away from the old homeland in Moscow. Here she lived in the house of her daughter Emma Auguste, who was married to Colonel Hermann Wilhelm **von Bock** and died on June 2 (14), 1856.

The portraits of the couple, painted in oil, are in Pommusch, in the possession of Gustav von Boetticher.

Outwardly cool and relaxed, Fritz had a warm and caring heart, and deep affection connected him with his siblings. He was proud of his brothers and their successes in their military careers. With every medal they received, he felt they were for him, too. But his interest was not only in his brothers. With the same love and kindness, he received his mother and the sisters who lived with him. This arrangement made him happy, and a close bond of love persisted, even if they lived far away, between all siblings.

Friedrich Wilhelm Heinrich Boetticher left behind the following sons and daughters:

1. **Johanna** Marie Elisabeth Eleonore, born in Tuckum, April 6 (18), 1809

2. **Emma** Auguste Philippine, born in Tuckum, August 26, (September 7), 1811

3. **Alexander** Friedrich Johann, born in Tuckum, December 10 (22), 1812

4. Moritz Carl **Oscar**, born in Tuckum, January 1 (13), 1814

5. **Johann** Carl Ernst, born in Tuckum, January 31 (February 12), 1816

6. **Gustav** Friedrich, born in Tuckum, August 10 (22), 1817

7. **Elisabeth** Eleonore, born in Tuckum, February 26 (March 10), 1819

8. **Friedrich** Carl Christoph, born in Tuckum March 18 (30), 1821

B.   (2) **Carl** Christoph Gottlieb von Boetticher (born in Goldingen, April 29, 1772; died in Petersburg, _____, 184___)

Carl Christoph Gottlieb, the second son of the court official **Johann** Christoph, was born in Goldingen where his father was city secretary on April 29 (May 11), 1772. Just like his younger brothers, Moritz and Gustav, he joined the army, where he received high honours. We will report about these three brothers, especially **Philipp Gustav**, but right now it is Carl's turn. At first, he went into the Polish Army, and in 1795, he held the rank of captain. Around this time, the Polish Army was dissolved and taken over by the Russian Empire. A year later, Carl entered the Russian Army. As a Captain with the Nowgorod Musketeer Regiment, he experienced the Second Coalitions War. Under the leadership of Suworow, the troops went through Galizien, Hungary, and the Steiermark (Austria) to Italy and from there marched across the St. Gotthard Pass to Switzerland to fight at the side of the Austrians to prevent a further invasion of the French and to prevent their takeover of Italy. Carl was much involved in the fight of the Genueser Mountains in July and August 1799. In the war near Novi, between Genua (Genoa) and Alessandria, on August 3 (15), he again took part. This was the bloodiest campaign of the war and ended with the defeat and withdrawal of the French. Italy seemed to be lost for the French as Suworow got the order to leave the Italian War to the Austrians and move to Switzerland to chase the French from this republic. So the Russian Army took part in the memorable move across the Alps into Switzerland. After repeated fights against French troops, under dangerous and difficult conditions, Carl crossed the St. Gotthard on September 13 (25). At the fight before the Urner Loch and the half-destroyed Teufelsbrücke, the enemy was pushed from its position and near Altdorf again defeated. Thereafter, the troops moved on small paths of the Schächen Valley and the Valley of Muotta to further march across the Pragelpass to Glarus. The difficulties the army experienced there were without precedent. Many soldiers died. Carl, with his great resistance, survived. But before Suworow's army reached Switzerland and the united Austrian and Russian troops there, the French had already been defeated and Suworow had to withdraw. In a meeting with the enemy on September 19 (31), Carl found a great opportunity to prove his military competence. The French were defeated and chased all the way to Schwyz. Carl showed great courage during this battle. He was wounded in his hand by an enemy bullet. His performance found the highest recognition, and later on, he received a medal. The Russian Army moved for the second time across the snow-covered Alps from Graubünden to get to Chur, Feldkirch, and Lindau and into the Rhine Valley. From there, Carl reached Bavaria, Bohemia, and Galizia and with his regiment went back to Russia. After a short rest, he was called back up again. During the Italian and Switzerland campaigns, he had no opportunity to send any news about himself to his family and they often thought he was dead. First they read in a Petersburg newspaper of his decoration, and then finally, in April 1800, a letter arrived from him in which he wrote in detail about his experiences. These left a great impression among his relatives, and in a letter from his younger brother Philipp in Mitau on July 30 (August 11), 1800, to him we read:

> Your destiny interests me very much and I am not sure if I should feel sorry or envy you. On the one side the tribulations you have experienced during the war must have been terrible and the loss of your troops weigh heavy on you. On the other side to be able to take part in a successful campaign that in this war was without parallel and the high contentment of our monarch which proves to you that you took part in the glorious deeds of our army and brought honour for Russia, makes up for it. Many had the opportunity to leave a mark, but only a few did. You are among the honourable few. We are especially happy that you reached fame without losing life or limbs and with you we thank the kind providence that saved you from the sad outcome many of your colleagues had.

The Third Coalition War brought Carl Boetticher, who was now major, again into foreign countries. Led by Prince Bagration, he marched through Galizien (Galicia) and Silesia into Austria. In forced marches, he reached the small town of Braunau in Bohemia, not far from the Prussian border on November 10 (22), 1805. On the days of the murderous battle near Austerlitz, November 20 (December 2),

1805, he fought at Schöngrobern in Lower Austria. Right after, he made the tough withdrawal, to which the disbursed army was forced after every battle. With his Nowgorod troops, Carl was ordered to move to Moldova and Wallachia.

The war against the French followed the war against the Turks, and the field and camp life that Carl had chosen continued. On November 12 (24), 1806, he was involved in the capture of Bender and in the following year in the siege of Ismail. Repeatedly he faced the enemy in the open field until the final peace of Bucharest on May 14 (28), 1812. Here the River Pruth became the border between Russia and Turkey, and the Russian troops moved back home to face Napoleon's massive army.

During the war against Turkey, in 1807, Carl was promoted to colonel, and in 1812, he was transferred to the Kurski Regiment. With this regiment, he stood at the lower Bug River when the Austrian-Saxonian army, led by Prince Schwarzenberg, crossed the border. On July 15 (27), he met with the enemy army, the Saxonians, led by Klengel, near Kobrin. Here the Russians captured 2000 men and eight canons. Not quite as lucky but undecided was the meeting near Gorodezno on July 31 (August 12). After the withdrawal of the French from Moscow, Carl fought Napoleon's army from November 14 to 16 (26–28) as they crossed Beresina. Near Borissow, at the Village Stachow, Carl once again faced the enemy bullets. He did not take part in the fights that opened the road for the Russian Army to Paris. In the year 1813, Carl had the task to form reserve divisions to be moved later to the active army. After the peace agreement, he was in charge of a garrison battalion, and later he had the position of commander of a brigade, the Inner Watch. In December 1833, he took his retirement as a major general but not before he had received different decorations, among them the Annenorden (Order of St. Anna), 2nd Class. He retired to his Courlandic homeland where he lived for many years peacefully. He finished his busy life in St. Petersburg on _____, 18___. From age 27 to 40, he was almost constantly involved in campaigns outside his country, so he never had the time for family life or to establish his own household. He stayed a bachelor, and this got him a closer connection to his siblings, especially to the district court lawyer Philipp Boetticher in Mitau with whom he had dreamed together in youth of a happy future. Did these dreams come true later in life? After the "wild roll of the iron dice", he experienced the totally different circumstances of peacetime! His diverse life happened at a time when the history of the people and nations of Europe was decided on the battlefields. He took part in these fights and used all his energy to do his best in this job that destiny had provided for him. And to have been there at the deciding hour for the good of the people must have given him much satisfaction, even though his life turned out different than he had dreamed in his youth. His portrait hangs in the home of the privy councillor Alexander von Boetticher in Riga.

B. (3) **Philipp** Gustav von Boetticher (born _____, 1775 in Tuckum; died April 5 (17), 1829 in Mitau).

Philipp Gustave was a district court advocate. The third son of the court official Johann Christoph Boetticher, Philipp was born in _____, 1775 in Tuckum. He studied law and went to the University of Jena in 1792. At the turn of the century, many significant professors taught at this university. This may have been the attraction for him and many other men from Courland. We know little about his time in the old city of entertainment or how well he did in his studies. But he must have used his time wisely in Jena, judging by the way he succeeded later in his profession. He also enjoyed the lively time of a student that Jena is known for even to this day. Repeated hikes, drives, and horseback rides to the nearby towns of Drakendorf, Triesnitz, and others around Jena kept him busy. Other times, on special occasions, he made a bigger tour to Rudolstadt for a masquerade or a great party in Weimar, "where," as he writes, "the men from Jena had their way with the Weimar ladies." Even with the success in Weimar, he and his friends held "a nightly court about all the ladies" and a get-together in his room.

From the olden days, it was customary in Jena that the professor was not only the teacher for the student in the classroom. Outside, too, he had contact with him, offered access to his family, and took personal interest in his activities, and this direct involvement often with significant personalities certainly helped to develop the overall intellect and the character of the younger man. Philipp too found among the professors, men with whom he connected. We know that he visited the well-known lawyer Gottfried Hufeland (1760–1817) often and that he was in the house of Professor Christian Gottfried Schütz (1747–1832), the founder of the first German Literatur newspaper repeatedly. "I find in his house," he writes about the last named, "everything that makes life better in Jena."

Philipp's outstanding intellectual personality, his charm and wit, and his cheerfulness may have gained him many friends. A surviving page of a family book shows a drawing of Prince Heinrich LXI von Reuss-Plauen with his signature and these words for Philipp: "People are not only connected when they are together, the far away too is close by. Hopefully your friend Heinrich LXI Reuss-Plauen is included. Jena on the 17th February 1804."

Like every other Jena student, Philipp too probably hated to leave the old city of entertainment on the River Saale and counted the memory of the times there as the best of his life.

In 1796, Philipp was back in his parents' house. While he had been away from home, many important changes had taken place. Peter Biron, the last Duke of Courland, had given up his reign. Courland was taken over by the Russian Empire in 1795, and soon after, Empress Katharine II established the Russian City Constitution. With the newly established eight classes and grades for the civil servants, Philipp landed a "small job," which netted him, with all part-time work, only 150 rubles a year. This was enough for him to live with his parents in Tuckum, and in his spare time, he was able to help his old father with his business. Philipp lived a rich life without worries in "his beloved Tuckum." His older brother Carl was with his regiment in Petersburg at that time. Moritz had just started his military career as Junker and was seldom seen back home. Gustav was in school with Probst Bitterling in Selzen. At home were the sisters Lieschen, Hennchen and Caroline and the oldest brother, Fritz. The contact with his siblings and parents and the friendly get-togethers with good friends in the country gave Philipp everything he needed to keep him happy. He wrote a letter from these times to his brother Carl in Petersburg to tell him about the life at home.

Mum and Dad are happy and healthy, they live as always in the circle of their good friends; they make trips into the country for a few days and then get back home to attend to the business that had collected while they were gone. Fritz and I go hunting and horseback riding. We each own a horse and now and again we go to a party, in short, we live good and happy. The sisters are quite busy, they sew shirts for me, knit socks and do what they are supposed to do in this world.

These happy times soon ended. On November 6 (17), 1796, the Empress Katharine died. Emperor Paul took the throne and shortly thereafter all the reforms of Empress Katharine in Courland were removed. This changed the country and city constitutions, and in the Baltic Sea provinces, he gave back the old knights country law. In this new environment, Philipp lost his civil servant position and was forced to look for a different job. His former department boss, Count Mendem, offered him a new position as a private secretary. Count Carl Johann Friedrich von Mendem was the older brother of the last Duchess of Courland, Anna Charlotte Dorothea, who was a very wise lady with great intellect. After her husband died in Löbichau in Altenburg County, she surrounded herself with scholars and artists. Count Mendem had a leading position in Courland. He was not only a large estate owner and government nobility leader; he was also admired by everyone as a noble-minded person. In Mitau and on his estates, he led an excellent household that he also kept in Petersburg. In his residence, as in the provincial city, the Count kept the finest company in which his wife Elisabeth (née Empire Duchess von Browne) was known to be endearing and graceful. Philipp was now part of this circle, and this must not have been an easy decision for him. With his nature, it was tough for him to be in a position of dependence, and also to lose his close connection to the family life with his parents and siblings must have hurt him. But the financial reimbursement of the count was, at that time, quite good and he could not refuse the offer. This high salary was soon raised again. The obligations in this new job for Philipp consisted of looking after the correspondence of the nobility leader and helping with the large business ventures and fortunes, including those of the Duchess of Courland. As private secretary, he had to take part in all of the Duke's activities and travel with him. He met all kinds of personalities, and these connections helped him greatly in later activities. The frequent visits to Petersburg he enjoyed very much, and he "admired the emperor city and all it had to offer." Philipp lived in these circumstances for four years, and even though it was not easy, he never regretted this move later in life. In a letter to his brother Carl in April 1797, shortly after starting his new position, he talks about his feelings and emotions.

I have everything I need, my salary is such that I can afford what I want; everything I get here is of the best. My Duke is very kind towards me and his wife is courteous. What else does one want to be happy? And still I find a certain uneasiness and emptiness in my heart. For everybody else in my position would be the quintessence of their wishes, but I wish for something different. For a long time I was used to be among friends and relatives and they enjoyed my good nature and sometimes encouraged me with a smile and had fun at social gatherings. Many a joke or hearty laughter I have to avoid now, instead I have to listen and smile, not that people ask me to, but I can read it in their eyes to better be quiet. But maybe this will change in the future. Right now I am homesick and all is new for me. If I'm here longer and get to know the people around me better, I hope to live more happily.

This hope seemed to have come true with his long stay in the Mendem house. In the letters home, Phillip gave his feelings free rein and showed his kind personality, and even one hundred years later, it is appropriate to open them to the reader. Among others, he writes to his brother Moritz on April 4, 1797:

For sending me your love, I thank you very much, being with my siblings at home with the parents, I enjoyed their love daily, but thought I had earned it; now that I'm away from all of them, I realize how much I miss them all. So every new proof of the continuing love of my loved ones is endlessly dear to me and is a natural result of my emotions right now.

But opening his heart this way was not enough. Philipp not only put his love into words, he also acted. In the same letter, we read further on:

Too bad you cannot be transferred to Mitau. We could have lived nicely together and helped you … your sickness hurts me. The care that a poor soldier receives is usually not the best, especially if he has no money, which seems to be the case with you. The fever is not a dangerous sickness, but one feels it a lot … Take the silver money that I send along, my dear brother, I demand it as proof of your love. I don't need it and you have better use for it. When you are General, you can return the gift in the form of a Tartar stallion.

A few years later, Philipp had the chance to help his brother Moritz again. To show the kind way, Philipp went about this, we repeat word for word this letter that he wrote to his brother Moritz on July 5, 1800.

I have to make a confession to you. The devil! Sir brother, that was a stupid trick of your Sir Valet, that not only I left but also absentminded took along your valet, when I packed up my things. Lacking brains can have real bad consequences! There the Lieutenant sat now, poorer than Hiob, chewed on his nails to think of a way to plug the hole in his finances. The natural way was, of course, with some money from a friend. But why did your genius not think of me? For this I cannot forgive you, but I will, if you let me make it up to you. I guessed correctly right away that our friend Schmidt must have been the one you went to and he had given you the money. After my investigation I found this to be true. So I asked our friend to take the money from me. But what happened? A few days ago I got a letter with a red shield that said you had paid him already and so quickly and here is your money back. Now I was in trouble. My account was closed, the sum paid to Schmidt already calculated in. The surplus now made a mess in my account and I needed to get rid of it so I decided to pack it up and send it to you. Perhaps you have use for it and you do me a favour by keeping this destroyer of my peace and quiet and you are not too proud to keep it, especially since you made the mistake not to ask me right away, so that I can forgive you … Let me know soon, dear boy, how you are. If you are happy and healthy and if you will soon get a promotion. Say hello to the dear cousin

Becker and his wife, that I, by the description I got of her, hold in high regard ...

In the previous letter to his brother Moritz, he not only showed his nice character trait in helping quickly, if possible, but in the way he went about it, how he carefully by avoiding all embarrassment for the receiver with the help of all possibilities made him take the help. His friendly and sincere way shines through in the following lines he wrote on July 30, 1800, to his brother Carl at the end of the Russian War against the French in the Second Coalitions War:

A feeling that I cannot explain got over me and with it I am writing to you, my dear, best loved brother Carl. After years that feel like an eternity to me, I am able to let my heart speak to you. How great this yearning of this conversation with you had been, your own feelings will tell you. Often when I had asked the parents for news about you, I got "We have not a line from him" and then the terrible thought hit me, "Carl is no more," and my heart was sad for the loss of my dear brotherly companion of my youth, with whom I had dreamt once of a happy future and still at the last goodbye, had hoped for more happy times together. At times, when we so scattered living siblings met at our dear parents', when we sat together and reminisced about old times and the funny events we had partaken together, we remembered you well and felt the gap that could never be closed. This hurt even more as we had doubts this gap would be closed. Between being hopeful and scared due to your very long silence, thinking of the worst, our fear left quickly when we read your name in the Petersburg newspaper and the medal that our Monarch had bestowed upon you. The name of the regiment and all other circumstances were correct, so we knew it was none other than our dear Carl, who had fought so bravely in Italy and now was rewarded. Now we knew you are alive and well and all we needed was a letter from you and after a long wait, this happened too. … It would be a waste of time to tell you about the emotions I felt reading your letter. I devoured every line—recognized you everywhere—thought as I read your letter you were talking—and as I was holding it, I felt I was giving you a hug. In short, I was in a state that in its form is special and only feeling minds will understand …

Carl Boetticher had written his family about the experiences he had during the campaign of the Russians under Suworow in Italy and across the St. Gotthard into Switzerland. On a different spot, Philipp writes in his letter to Carl about the very hard and difficult times he must have had to endure. It was important to us here to show the personality of the kind writer in his own words and to characterize him for the generations to come. Unfortunately, so far only a few letters of his later life could be found, and this makes it impossible to know exactly his life story, regarding the heart and soul of this so very knowledgeable, generous-minded man.

After Philipp had terminated his position with Duke Medem, he prepared himself to become an advocate. By order of Justice Minister Prince Lapuchin on October 26 (November 7), 1805, he was appointed as lower court lawyer, and on November 20 (December 2) of the same year, he took the oath. By resolution of the Mitau District Court from February 26 (March 10), 1807, he got the appointment to district court lawyer, and in this position, he worked until the end of the life. This kept him in Mitau. Here he had his extended practice because not only did the large circle of the Courlandic nobility give him their trust, but he was admired by many and had numerous friends.

In 1814, he met a young lady whom he got to know better and whose lovely picture found its way to his heart. She was Helene von Reichard, born December 10 (22), 1796. Philipp decided to send someone to ask for her hand in marriage and then waited impatiently to see how his future would be decided. He informed his siblings about this situation and wrote to a brother:

What fascinates me about Helene Reichard, you know yourself, because I think you were in love with her just like me at the time when we both met her. But as you "fled" and perhaps forgot about her and have changed your taste a dozen times since ... the little spark in me became a flame. The offer to her was made by a third person to the daughter. Her parents know about it, and I have the approval from them. But I made the offer to her acting as if her parents have no idea, because I want her free decision for her yes.

Philipp was not kept in the dark for long as to how the dice had been rolled. He received the yes that changed his life. The previous writer of many letters to his siblings now had to apologize to them for not writing. He let them know that he had a totally different correspondence, which took all his time, and that was with his bride. His busy office let him get away only every two weeks for a few days to visit his bride in Riga, and when he got back, the work had piled up. Under these circumstances, he assured his loved ones at home that he had not forgotten them. He asked them just not to throw stones at him because he had so little time for them. He was happy every time he had the opportunity to experience "the modest kindness of his bride" and realized soon that she would fit well into his family to become a loving member and get along with them all. The wedding took place in the spring of 1815 on the Estate Paddern, and at Johanni, he was in his nice house even though he was quite busy at that time of year and enjoyed the comfort. He did not complain anymore about all the people who came to visit as he had before but instead wrote to a brother that his Helene always had room for many nice guests; at Johanni, she took in six—his mother-in-law, his brother-in-law Carl Sivers, his brothers Carl and Fritz, and his sister Caroline. "Of course my dearest was quite busy in the kitchen everyday now and I had missed the celebrations around Johanni, which are special for young married couples and the nice honeymoon I was able to enjoy only half because of the ever-pressing workload. But then, what is a honeymoon," Philipp writes, "a whole beautiful life lays ahead of me. My Helene is really a good, dear wife and every day I discover new, nice characteristics and so grows closer to my heart ... I'm also very pleased that she is well liked everywhere, wherever she goes, which is important in Mitau, where people are suspicious toward newcomers and that says a lot."

Philipp, who had such plans for a rich, happy life, had no idea that it would end early. During his steady working life, he took only a few days off for rest and recuperation, and this was wrong for his weak constitution. He was happy after the Johanni business was done to take a few weeks off with his relatives and enjoy the sea and beach at Baldohn. He had little time for pleasures. The nice team of horses, which his horse-loving brother Moritz had gotten for him (they were supposed to be the most beautiful horses in Mitau), got less exercise than they needed. Trips into foreign countries at that time were not made as often as they are now. It is not known if Philipp and his family ever crossed the border, but during the summertime, they visited their friends and relatives in Courland and Livland who lived in the country, and Philipp wrote his brother Moritz on September 6, 1818, about his pleasure tours to Riga, Doblen, Baldohn, Gouverneurs–Hof, Tuckum and Plahnen. These were blessed with beautiful weather and were good for his health, since for a few days, his chest and stomach felt better after these tours.

These mentioned ailments at first did not keep him away from the good times at home. His wife gave birth to two sons and numerous daughters, and under the watchful eyes of their parents, they all grew up nicely. A good drawing (in possession of States Councillor Theodor von Boetticher) shows the lucky family father and on his side, his Helene, both surrounded by sons and daughters with their still soft features. In the fine statures of especially two daughters, we can see already how well they will develop later on. If one looks closely at the face of the father, one sees a man of great talent and spirit who impressed everyone who was lucky enough to have met him. From his previous letters, we know how friendly Philipp was towards others and how willingly he put the interests of other people before his own. The amount and diversity of work that as district court lawyer he was trusted with, shows his significance to us. To characterize how Philipp thought of the important political happenings during his time, we add one more letter, which deals with relevant questions. He writes in June 1815,

Yesterday the authentic news arrived here by courier that Bonaparte had lost his throne and was arrested and that Paris has a new government led by Ludwig the XVIII under Macdonald's and Qudinot's leadership. We wait for more details. Perhaps he had fled to Paris after the deciding lost battle against Wellington and Blücher to start a new revolution but met the end there by the hands of his own supporters. The talk is, for a while now, that our guard and Wittgensteins Corps had gotten orders to stop. Unbelievable things we experience in our days and the last event is no less surprising than the previous one. The triumphant return from the Island of Elba to Paris and on the throne, all this ended by losing the one battle. With God's help, we now have peace for good after this monster that nobody should let go has been defeated.

The chest pain that Philipp had complained about in previous years got worse over time. He would have liked to take a spa treatment in Germany, but important business did not allow for this. The thought of a visit to Carlsbad or any other good spa was quite intriguing to him since this would have brought him back to the "lovely Germany, where I had spent such happy times." He had to forget this idea and take the medicine that "the dear Fatherland has to offer." But those brought no relief. In the year 1824, he slowly got weaker, and beginning in 1829, he often had to stay in bed. If he would just slow down a little! But his work continued, and letters that he was unable to write, he dictated for others.

He died half an hour before midnight on April 5 (17), 1829, at 54 years old, after a very busy life. His widow thanked him "for the short 14 years of marriage and the most beautiful life she had with him. This gave her the faith and devotion to carry on after the irreplaceable loss to be there for the children that God had left her."

Die Freunde liebte er mit reiner Herzens weihe,
Ohn' Eigennutz und frei von allem Scheine,
Mit edler Freiheit und mit fester Treue,
Doch Worte waren's nicht, das Herz muss drunter sein.

Those were the meaningful words that the widow, the relatives, and numerous friends had added to the obituary. His friends expressed their feelings with the following words:

So scheiden denn die Freunde, Einer nach dem Andern;

Es ist des Pilgers Loos: er muss hienieden wandern

Bis er das Ziel erreicht. Das Ziel? Es ist das Grab.

Den Einen zieht es früh, den Andern spät hinab.

Voll Müh' und Sorge ist der Lauf zum Ziele,

Drum klaget nicht um den, der früher es erreicht—

Er schlummert nach des sauren Tages Schwüle.

Jetzt sanft und ruhig in des Abends Kühle

Wo jede Sorge nun und jedes Leiden schweigt;

Drum wünscht nur noch dem Freund:

Die Erde sei ihm leicht.

Ave pia anima!

Philipp Gustav von Boetticher and Helene (née von Reichard) had eight children of which four passed away before their father did. Here are the names of the four children who survived him:

1. Carl Johann **Theodor** von Boetticher, born September 28 (October 10), 1819, in Mitau, the Russian emperor's privy councillor

2. **Clara**, born March 15 (27), 1822, in Mitau; died January 22 (February 3), 1888 in Dresden, married to the Russian emperor privy councillor Nicolaus Baron von Tornauw

3. **Helene**, born September 21 (October 3), 1833, in Mitau, married to the Russian emperor's consul and states councillor Carl Alexander von Radetzky-Mikulicz

4. Gustav Eduard **Philipp**, born September 23 (October 5), 1825, in Mitau; died May 1 (13), 1849, in Riga, a Russian emperor lieutenant engineer

B. (4) **Moritz** Johann Ernst von Boetticher (born in Tuckum May 11 (23), 1777; died in Wenden April 3 (15), 1848).

Moritz Johann Ernst, the fourth son of the court official **Johann** Christoph Boetticher, joined the army in 1796. He was promoted to officer candidate of the Sophia Musketeer Regiment in September 1798 and second lieutenant in October of the following year. By October 1803, he was a first lieutenant. He received this quick advancement because he showed great enthusiasm and was conscientious in his daily tasks. When he was still an officer candidate, just like any regular soldier, he had to get ready with all the equipment for a march and he thought it a point of honour to carry everything himself, so that nobody got the idea that a Russian was superior to a German when it came to taking the strain. Other officer candidates let the soldiers carry their heavy rifles and luggage.

After Moritz had been promoted to staff captain in October 1806 and had moved to the Kaluga Regiment, he took part in the campaign at the eastern border of Prussia at the end of 1806 and in the following year. After the capture of Danzig, the Russian Army left its position between Alle and Pregel. The unlucky meeting near Heilsberg on May 29 (June 10), 1807, made the Russian Army decide to pull back from the battlefields. Near Königsberg, the last uncaptured city of the Prussian monarch, there were also some fights until the troops pulled back and the French took over. After the Tilsit Peace Treaty, the army left the southwestern border of the empire to be employed in Finland. Under the leadership of Buxhöwden, the army moved into Finland, and the conquest of that country went quickly. Near the church of Lappo on July 2 (14), 1808, and near Kuortane on August 20 (September 1), 1808, it came to bloody battles with the Swedish troops. For his daring bravery near Kuortane, Moritz received the Annenorden, 4th Class. He fought in the Battle of Hednafors on June 23 (July 5), 1809, and in the fight near Ratan on August 8 (20), 1809. Both times he was wounded in the foot, and this made him decide to put his military career on hold for a while. After the battle near Hednafors, he was recommended for the "monarch benevolent" for his bravery and enthusiasm. After the fight near Ratan, he was promoted to captain and received the Wladimir Medal, 4th Class. On December 20 (January 1), 1810/11, he left the service as a major with a uniform and an invalid's pension.

During the happenings of the year 1812, Moritz was unable to watch from the outside. He had recuperated, and this made it possible for him to enter the service once again. He entered in his former rank as captain into the Riga Dragoner Regiment and was appointed adjutant to the General of Cavalry, His Majesty the Duke Alexander von Württemberg. His relations to this superior were decisive for his future life. Not only during the war but also in the following time of peace, Moritz was as an attaché, closely connected to the Duke and was his steady companion during all his campaigns and travels. From July 13 to 15 (25–27), he took part in the fights near Witebsk and was in the rearguard at the retreat from Witebsk to Smolensk under daily bombardment. From August 5 to 7 (17–19) near Smolensk, under the command of Duke Alexander von Württemberg, he got the order to deliver instructions for the army leader Barclay de Tolly to some of the most dangerous front positions. On August 17 (29), he fought in the battle near Wyäsma and on August 24 (September 5) was in the murderous battle of Borodino in the corps of General Dochturow. For his proven courage and prudence in these fights, he was awarded the Annenorden 2nd Class. At the following larger and smaller battles, first at the retreat of the Russian Army and then at the ousting of the French, he was always fully engaged by Tarutino on October 5 and 6 (17 and 18) and near Malo-Jaroslawetz on October 12 (24) and the conquering of the city of Gshatsk on August 20 (September 1). On

October 30 (November 11), 1812, he had orders to join the troops of the Cossacks' leader, Duke Plastow, for a while and was, until the conquest of Wilna at the end of November, engaged in different battles. After that, he went back to his previous posting and was from February 1813 on in the Dukedom Warschau. In the spring, he moved outside of Danzig where Napoleon had stationed a large part of his troops who had gotten away from Russia and arrived there in April 1813 under the leadership of Duke Alexander von Württemberg to blockade the fortress with his corps. For his proven bravery in the fights of Malo-Jaroslawetz on May 18 (30), 1813, and the ousting of the enemy army, he was promoted to major, and after winning the battle in the last assault of the French on May 28 (June 9), 1813, he was recognized by the highest authority for his bravery and the orders he had given. From his monarch, he received the Golden Saber with the inscription "for bravery," and the King of Prussia sent him a document with the medal "Pour le Mérite." Shortly thereafter, at the conquest of the Danzig suburb Langefuhr, where he showed great bravery, he was promoted to lieutenant colonel. After the capitulation of Danzig at the end of 1813, he got the honourable order to bring the news of the victory to St. Petersburg. With this, he ends his service in the army. Moritz was promoted to colonel in 1823. He now held the position of a civil servant for special orders of Duke Alexander von Württemberg. Of the different decorations that he had received, we have to mention the Medal of the Holy Georg, 4th Class, for 25 years of excellent service as an officer in the year 1823. He was also rewarded the diamonds to the Annenorden, 2nd Class in 1826. And lastly, he received the silver medal commemorating the year 1812.

On his request, Moritz was released from duty with a full pension and the right to wear the uniform in January 1836. He lived the last years of his life in the City of Wenden in the Province of Livland where he died on April 3 (15), 1848. An iron cross on the cemetery of Wenden shows his last resting place.

Moritz was not married. People who knew him remember him as having an imposing stature and a friendly nature. He had been a soldier, body and mind, but he also loved art and decorated his home with the works of art. This hobby succeeded by far that of a regular cavalry officer. Until the end of his life, he was close to Duke Alexander von Württemberg, whom he held in deep affection and admiration, and his former war leader always remembered him fondly. Two portraits from his estate, owned by the privy councillor Alexander von Boetticher in Riga, show the imposing statures of him and the Duke.

B.   (5) **Gustav** Ernst von Boetticher (born _____, 1782, in Tuckum; died in St. Petersburg on December 20, 1847 (January 1, 1848)).

Gustav Ernst, the fifth son of the court official in Tuckum **Johann** Christoph Boetticher, baptized February 22 (March 6), 1782, chose, just like his brothers Carl and Moritz, a life in the military. He joined the army in 1807 and was a lieutenant in the same year in the First Pionier Regiment. The war in Finland in the years 1808–1809 gave him many opportunities to get experiences in the art of siege war and to prove himself as a brave officer. After the siege of Swartholm and the affaire near Helsingfors on February 18 (May 2), 1808, he fought under the Engineer General Duke Suchtelen before Sweaborg, the Gibraltar of the north. At the conquering of the fortress on April 22 (May 4), 1808, he showed great bravery and received the Annenorden, 4th Class. In 1810, he was appointed adjutant to Major General Schwanenbach and soon switched this position to become adjutant to the General of Cavalry, Duke Alexander von Württemberg. He stayed in this position even after he was transferred to the Taurisch Grenadier Regiment in February 1812 and promoted to staff captain. From June 1812, Gustav fought against the large Napoleonic army. In the battle near Witebsk, July 13–15 (25–27), Commanding General Duke Ostermann-Tolstoy used him to take orders to the most dangerous positions of the front. During the three-day battle near Smolensk, August 5–17 (12–14), he fought with the corps of Prince Eugen von Württemberg and did the same service for the army leader Barclay de Tolly as he did near Witebsk under Duke

Ostermann. In these battles, as in the fight near Wjäsma (August 17 (29)) and in the Battle of Borodino (August 26 (September 7)), he was in the greatest danger. His performance and service were rewarded with the Wladmir Medal, 4th Class, with band. After he had fought near Tarutino on October 6 (18), he was transferred to the Cossack leader Duke Platow on October 10 (22) to take part in the battle near Malo-Jaroslawetz, which occurred on October 12 (24), and in the same month, under the orders of Major General Ilowaiski with 6000 Cossack soldiers, stormed into the back of the enemy, thereby capturing three squadrons of enemy cavalry and 17 cannons. The enemy was pushed back to Borodino, chased from the Abbey Polozk, which they had built as fortress, and forced to retreat from Gshatsk and Wjäsma. For his efforts, he was promoted to captain in the fall of 1812. Near Polozk, he was wounded on the left side. But this did not prevent him from taking part in the battles later on. Only after the pursuit of the enemy to Wilna did he collapse. He was very sick and had to stay behind, during which time the Russian troops moved victorious to the Prussian and Polish border.

In the beginning of the year 1813, Gustav was back again with his regiment in the Dukedom of Warschau. From there, they moved to Danzig in April where the French troops had dug in and with a blockade were forced to give up the city. During a rally by the French on May 28 (June 9), 1813, Gustav had the opportunity to show his skill. For this bravery, the monarch awarded him with the Golden Saber with the inscription "for bravery" and the King of Prussia decorated him with the medal "Pour le Mérite" for his efforts.

The main part of the Russian troops moved further west now, but Gustav, under the leadership of Duke Alexander von Württemberg, had to stay back near Danzig and fight the less glorious fortress war. He fought the enemy repeatedly, and for his bravery, he received the Annenorden with diamond jewelry. After the capitulation of Danzig in the fall of 1813, he was awarded the great honour of taking the news of victory to the Kaiser. At this time, the monarch promoted him to colonel and transferred him to the Semenow Garde Regiment.

From a letter written by the district court attorney Philipp von Boetticher to his brother, our Gustav, dated in Mitau, December 10 (22), 1813, we quote lines showing the close connection between the siblings and talking about the joy his brother had that Gustav had had such success and had been greatly rewarded. It also shows how eagerly everyone awaited the handing over of the City of Danzig because this was a first-class fortress with a depot for all war materials. He writes:

> You my dear brother made me very happy and this was even better by the choice of your letter carrier when I received your last letter. You can imagine how Caroline (his sister) and I were surprised when our dear Moritz arrived here. We had

heard about Danzig's capitulation but the official news was still missing and that one of you would deliver this news we had hoped very much, but nobody was sure. Now it was both of you that carried this happy news to the East and West. This is a very great award and I send my heartfelt congratulations to you. This high honour gave you the opportunity for an interesting trip but also the even greater award that you received there. For Moritz it was a nice gift to be able to visit us but the far better reward he got from Mother Empress. We are eager to know what you have received. We really think that the King of Prussia was very pleased since he is in possession of Danzig again. And our Alexander was very much involved in this campaign. Yes, we even remember that the Austrian too felt good about this and may reward you. When Moritz returns, you will probably arrive also and then let us not wait any longer.

After the capitulation of Danzig, camp life ended for a while for Gustav. In 1817, he was promoted commander of the 14th Rifleman Corps and advanced to major general in 1822. As such, he became commander for the 2nd Brigade of the 3rd Infantry Division. But in the year 1826, he received the command of the 3rd Brigade of the 7th Infantry Division. The year 1826 saw him back in battle. In the war against Turkey, 1828–1829, under Wittgenstein, he was with the Corps of Duke Eugen von Württemberg and appointed commander of the 2nd Brigade, 18th Infantry Division. He took part in the battles before Varna, which capitulated on September 29 (October 11), 1828, was involved in the siege of Schumla, and led other operations with much skill and success. Duke Eugen remembers our Gustav a few times in his memoirs about this campaign. The Duke was in the company of his cousins Alexander and Ernst von Württemberg during this war. In mentioning the success of the Russians against the attacking Turks near Schumla, he writes, "Alexander and Ernst were cutting down the enemy mightily with their sabres, behind them Mr. General Boetticher, their mentor and protector against youthful mistakes, was directing them during the fight." At the town of Marasch, south of Schumla, a fight took place, where "General Boetticher with the Perm Regiment and four cannons were moving through town to chase the Turks from the opposite valley." After the battle near Marasch, Prince Alexander had to leave the army because he got sick. Prince Ernst went along with him. "They were followed by the faithful Boetticher ... Now everything was ready for the trip to leave when the outrageous Turks attacked a transport near Jenibazar. Boetticher and the Marquis (a French man in the entourage of the Duke Eugen) loudly discussed the situation and that it be inexcusable to let the Prince leave without proper protection ..."

Even though these are only a few words that Duke Eugen uses to remember Gustav, the content shows us the connection that they had with each other.

Decorated with the Wladimir Medal, 3rd Class, and the George Cross, Gustav came back to Russia in 1828 where he found new activity a few years after. In February 1831, he was appointed inspector at the Engineer School for Road Communication in Petersburg. Now he had the opportunity to move into his residence and spend time with friends and family and to enjoy a social life. The new field of his activity at the Engineer School suited him well. He was married to **Eugenie** Pauline von Rosenschild and had the joy of raising two lovely daughters and one promising son. His daughters both married in Petersburg. One of them, **Elise**, got married to Lieutenant General von Peretz, in charge of the Mountain Corps. The other, **Leontine**, married Lieutenant General and Division Commander von Nabél. His son, **Adolf**, served with the Moskau Guard Regiment and was already a staff captain in 1849 when the Russians supported the Austrians in a campaign against the Hungarians. In the town of Swenziany in the Province of Wilna, he got sick in an epidemic and died early in life.

Gustav von Boetticher received the Stanislaus Medal, 1st Class, in the year 1831 and a grant of a so-called arrende (a pay raise of 1000 rubles), a new sign of goodwill by his monarch. Transferred into civil life, he had the rank of a privy council.

He died in St. Petersburg on December 20 (January 1), 1848, at the age of 65. We study his picture with admiration in a life-size oil portrait owned by the privy council Alexander von Boetticher in Riga.

C.

Relations by Marriage of the von Boetticher Family with Other Families Since Their Appearance in Courland

• • •

A. **Families from which the Boettichers Chose Their Wives**

Baumgarten, Baroness von Behr, von Bidder, von Boetticher, von Brutzer, Deringer, Dienstmann, von Friede, Goetecke, von Haudring, Havenstein, Heisler, von Hollander, Kriloff, Kurow, von Kurowski, von Latzki, Melnitzky, von Mirbach, Mitschke, Baroness von d. Osten-Sacken, Pander, Paulin von Rosenschild, Poorten, Preschkow, Pusin, von Reichard, Reiss, von Roques, San-Galli, von Sengbusch, von Tallberg, Tarakanow, Thoms, Trapesnikoff, Trawin, Vorkampff-Laue, Wilpert, Wippert, von Wippermann

B. **Families into which Boetticher Daughters Married**

Becker, Bergengruen, von Bidder, von Bilterling, von Bock, von Boetticher, Curti, Drachenhauer, Gamper, Gundling,

Jassinsky, Kawen, Kerkowius, von Krannhals, Kreysern, Kühn, Lösevitz, von Nabél, Pabst, von Pacht, von Peretz, von Radetzky-Mikulicz, Popow, Reiss, Skolon, Sommer, Strojew, Baroness von Tornauw, Wassiliew, Winziger

Family Register Information

On September 1, 1891

<u>Personal State</u>

I.	Male members	51
II.	Unmarried Boetticher daughters	19
III.	Married and widowed Boetticher daughters	17
IV.	Boetticher wives and widows	<u>17</u>
	Together	104

Personal News

I. Male Members

1. **Alexander** Friedrich Johann von Boetticher, son who in July 1831† Court Official **Friedrich** Wilhelm Heinrich von Boetticher and who on June 2 (14), 1856 † married **Agnes** Anna (née Pusin); he was a Royal Russian engineer, privy councillor and knight, excellence. He was born on December 10 (22), 1812, in Tuckum and was married to Agnes on October 7 (18), 1820, and died December 8 (20), 1883 † Baroness Feodora von der Osten-Sacken—Riga

2. Carl Johann **Theodor** von Boetticher, son of April 5 (17), 1829†, District Court Advocate Philipp Gustav von Boetticher, and on February7 (19), 1876† **Helene** (née von Reichard); Royal Russian States Councillor Retired, born September 28 (10 October), 1819, in Mitau; he was married to her on December 10 (22), 1818, born and March 20 (April 1), 1849† Agnes **Marie** (née Wilpert), II) with her on September2 (14), 1831, and on November3 (15), 1881†, Elise (nee von Boetticher), a sister of I, 4—Bauske

3. **Friedrich** Carl Christoph von Boetticher, brother of I, 1; Royal Russian staff officer retired, born March 18 (30), 1821 in Tuckum; (wife see under IV, 2)—Riga

4. **Friedrich** Heinrich von Boetticher, son of September 6 (18), 1859†, councillor and estate owner **Carl** Heinrich Johann von Boetticher and on September 14 (26), 1855†, **Emilie** Constantie (née Wippert); art historian, born June 11 (23), 1826, in Riga, was married I) to her on November 28 (December 10), 1826, born and on May 21 (June 2), 1858†; **Eugenie** (née Mitschke); (II. wife see under IV, 3)—Dresden

5. **Carl** Johann Ferdinand von Boetticher, son of the March 30 (April 11), 1855†, knights manor owner **Johann** Christoph Ernst von Boetticher, and on March 26 (April 7), 1830†; Helene **Mathilde** (née Poorten); owned the knights manors of Grenzhof and Dexten, retired, born January 30 (February 11), 1830, in Kuckschen; was married with her on May 20 (June 1), 1838, born and on December 5 (17), 1881†; **Wilhelmine** (née Brutzer)—Doblen

6. **Theodor** Philipp von Boetticher, brother of I, 4; knights manor owner of Great Spirgen in Courland and Dsernowitz in Province Witebsk; born April 7 (19), 1830, in Riga; wife see under IV, 4)—Great Spirgen

7. Carl **Oscar** von Boetticher, brother of I, 4; director of the Riga City Fire Insurance Company Ltd. and estate owner of Ebelshof and Lievenhof in Livland, born August 23 (September 4), 1835, in Ebelshof (wife see under IV, 5)—Ebelshof

8. **Emil** Friedrich von Boetticher, brother of I, 4; later mayor, now councillor in Riga, born October 1 (13), 1836, in Riga; was married I) with her on July 3 (15), 1841, born and on November 27 (December 9), 1871†; Christine (**Christel**) Albertine (née von Hollander) (II. wife see under IF, 6)—Riga

9. **Friedrich** Wilhelm Alexander von Boetticher, son of I, 1; Royal Russian States Councillor, Director of the Warschau Commerce School, Knight, born March 8 (20), 1839, in Goldingen (Wife see under IV, 7)—Warschau

10. **Rudolf** Johann Heinrich von Boetticher, brother of I, 5 from the second marriage and on March 30 (April 11), 1855† **Johann** Christoph Ernst von Boetticher (his II. wife see under IV, 1); knights manor owner of Kuckschen in Courland, born December 31, 1842 (January 12, 1843) in Kuckschen (wife see under IV, 8)—Kuckschen

11. **Victor** Carl Moritz von Boetticher, son of I, 1; Royal Russian Court Councillor, Chancellor Director of the Mitau Train Board of Directors, Knight, born November 4 (16), 1842, in Telechany Province Minsk (wife see under IV, 10)—Riga

12. **Paul** Eduard Alfred von Boetticher, son of I, 1; Royal Russian Court Councillor, Knight, civil servant for the Justice Ministry, born June 28 (July 10), 1846, in Telechany, Province Minsk (wife see under IV, 13)—St. Petersburg

13. **Gustav** von Boetticher, son of I, 2; doctor of law, previous court advocate in Riga, born March 15 (27), 1849, in Riga (wife see under IV, 9)—Odessa

14. **Walter** von Boetticher, son of I, 4; doctor of medicine, born November 29 (December 11), 1853, in Riga (wife see under IV, II)—Göda near Bautzen

15. **Gustav** Friedrich von Boetticher, son of July 6 (18), 1884†, knight manor owner, **Carl** Gustav Joseph von Boetticher and the March 30 (11 April), 1890†, **Adelheid** (née Baumgarten); Royal Russian Cavalry lieutenant, retired; knight, heir of Pommusch, born July 27 (August 8), 1854, in Pommusch, Courland (wife see under IV, 14)—Pommusch

16. Theodor **Ernst** von Boetticher, son of I, 6; jurist candidate, secretary at the city hall in Riga, born November 28 (December 10), 1858, in Ebelshof—Riga

17. **Oscar** Friedrich von Boetticher, son of I, 6; worked his father's estate Dsernowitz, born December14 (26), 1861, in Spirgen—Dsernowitz

18. **Hugo** Friedrich von Boetticher, son of I, 6; jurist candidate, works at the district court in Moskau, born October 1 (13), 1864, in Spirgen—Moskau

19. **Carl** Johann Friedrich von Boetticher, son of I, 5; jurist candidate, works at the district court in Kaluga, born May 23 (June 4), 1865, in Grenzhof—Kaluga

20. **Hermann** Carl von Boetticher, son of I, 6; Royal Russian lieutenant of reserve at Sappeuren, tenant of Nogallen in Courland, born March 29 (April 10), 1866 in Spirgen—Nogallen

21. Carl **Friedrich** Albert von Boetticher, son of I, 8; jurist candidate, at this time student of law in Leipzig, born September 14 (22), 1866, in Ebelshof—Leipzig

22. **Gustav** Alexander von Boetticher, son of I, 6; Royal Russian lieutenant, reserve with the dragoons, farmer, born September 10 (22), 1867, in Spirgen—Kowno

23. **Theodor** Oscar von Boetticher, son of I, 6; medical student in Dorpat, born January 16 (28), 1869, in Spirgen—Dorpat

24. **Johann** Christoph von Boetticher, brother of I, 15; forester of Castle Smilten in Livland, born September 26 (October 8), 1869, in Pommusch—Castle Smilten

25. **Bernhard** August von Boetticher, son of I, 5; born August 20 (September 1), 1870, in Autzenbach—Riga

26. **Oscar** Eduard Carl Henry von Boetticher, son of I, 7; born June 29 (July 11), 1874, in Ebelshof—Ebelshof

27. **Konrad** Wilhelm Erich von Boetticher, son of I, 6; born January 7 (19), 1875, in Spirgen—Riga

28. **Curt** Alexander Robert von Boetticher, son of I, 11; born April 25 (May 7), 1876, in Riga—Riga

29. **Herbert** Emil Theodor George von Boetticher, son of I, 7; born May16 (28), 1876, in Ebelshof—Ebelshof

30. **Carl** Heinrich Theodor von Boetticher, son I, 6; born June 27 (July 9), 1876, in Spirgen—Doblen

31. **Friedrich** Wilhelm Alduin Johann von Boetticher, son of I, 10; born October 26 (November 7), 1876, in Kukschen—Mitau

32. **Rudolph** Wilhelm Ernst von Boetticher, son of I, 5; born January 23 (February 4), 1878, in Gross-Blieden—Doblen

33. **Georg** Carl Alexander von Boetticher, son of I, 10; born September 12 (24), 1878, in Kuckschen—Mitau

34. **Theodor** Philipp Ottomar von Boetticher, son of I, 13; born June 4 (16), 1879, in Riga—Riga

35. **Erich** Gustav von Boetticher, son of I, 13; born May 28 (June 9), 1880, in Riga—Riga

36. **Friedrich** von Boetticher, son of I, 14; born October 2 (14), 1881, in Berthelsdorf in Saxony—Bautzen

37. **Adalbert** Franz Paul Alexander von Boetticher, son of I, 12; born August 1 (13), 1884, in St. Petersburg—St. Petersburg

38. Theodor **Wilhelm** von Boetticher, son that on September 10 (22), 1885†, estate owner of Stephanpol, Province Wilna, **Wilhelm**

Carl Friedrich von Boetticher (his wife see under IV, 12); born September 22 (October 4), 1884, in Stephanpol—Stephanpol

39. **Wolfgang** Rudolph Johann Heinrich von Boetticher, son of I, 10; born October 6 (18), 1885, in Kuckschen—Kuchschen

40. **Wolfgang** von Boetticher, son of I, 14; born December 6 (18), 1885, in Kötzschenbroda i. Saxony—Göda

41. **Hans** Franz Paul Friedrich von Boetticher, son of I, 12; born August 18 (30), 1886, in St. Petersburg—St. Petersburg

42. **Erich** Carl Walther von Boetticher, son of I, 15; born April 13 (25), 1889, in Pommusch—Pommusch

43. **Adalbert** von Boetticher, son of I, 14; born February 7 (19), 1889, in Dresden—Göda

44. **Werner** Wilhelm von Boetticher, son I, 15; born May 16 (28), 1890, in Pommusch—Pommusch

45. **Oscar** von Boetticher, son that on October 16 (28), 1875†; Royal Russian Staff Officer **Gustav** Friedrich von Boetticher (his wife see under IV, 15); Royal Russian Military Senior Physician, born January 19 (31), 1853 (Wife see under IV, 16)—Kostroma

46. **Theodor** von Boetticher, brother of I, 45; Royal Russian second lieutenant, born June 19 (July 1), 1864, in Rshew

47. **Nicolai** von Boetticher, brother of I, 45; Royal Russian second lieutenant, born May 6 (18), 1867, in Rshew (wife see under IV, 17)

48. **Georg** von Boetticher, son of I, 45; born January 22 (February 3), 1883, in Kostroma—Kostroma

49. **Nicolai** von Boetticher, son of I, 45; born January 15 (27), 1884, in Kostroma—Kostroma

50. **Wladimir** von Boetticher, son of I, 45; born March 2 (14), 1889, in Kostroma—Kostroma

51. **Boris** von Boetticher, son of I, 45; born May 14 (26), 1890, in Kostroma—Kostroma

II. Unmarried Boetticher Daughters

1. **Johanna** Maria Elisabeth Eleonore von Boetticher, sister of I, 1; born April 6 (18), 1809, in Tuckum—Riga†

2. **Elisabeth** Eleonore von Boetticher, sister of I, 1; born February 26 (March 10), 1819, in Tuckum—Riga† 1897

3. **Emmy** Maria Wilhelmine von Boetticher, daughter of I, 1; born October 3 (15), 1855, in Grodno—Riga

4. **Therese** Adele von Boetticher, sister of I, 15; born September 8 (20), 1863, in Pommusch—Pankelhof

5. **Elisabeth** Thecla von Boetticher, daughter of I, 5; born April 5 (17), 1867, in Grenzhof—Doblen

6. Polly **Marie** Emilie von Boetticher, daughter of I, 8; born May 20 (June 1), 1867, in Riga—Riga

7. **Wilhelmine** Helene von Boetticher, daughter of I, 6; born November 4 (16), 1870, in Spirgen—Spirgen

8. **Angelika** Auguste Emmy von Boetticher, daughter of I, 9; born January 23 (February 4), 1871, in Warschau—Warschau

9. **Marie** Henriette Pauline von Boetticher, daughter of I, 5; born May 23 (June 4), 1876, in Riga—Doblen

10. Anna **Alexandra** von Boetticher, daughter of I, 6; born July 3 (15), 1878, in Spirgen—Spirgen

11. **Anna** Victorine Hermine von Boetticher, daughter of I, 11; born January 5 (17), 1879 in Warschau—Riga

12. Lina **Grace** Anna Marie von Boetticher, daughter of I, 7; born May 20 (June 1), 1879, in Ebelshof—Ebelshof

13. **Elisabeth** Catharina von Boetticher, daughter of I, 6; born April 2 (14), 1880, in Spirgen—Spirgen

14. **Margarethe** Emmy Doris von Boetticher, daughter of I, 11; born April 17 (29), 1881, in Warschau—Riga

15. **Ilse** Sophie Maria von Boetticher, daughter of I, 12; born October 11 (23), 1882, in St. Petersburg—St. Petersburg

16. **Wilhelmine** Alexandra von Boetticher, daughter that on September 10 (22), 1885†; **Wilhelm** Carl Friedrich (wife see under IV, 12); born July1 (13), 1883, in Stephanpol—Stephanpol

17. **Dagmar** Agnes Maria von Boetticher, daughter of I, 12; born August 10 (22), 1883, in St. Petersburg—St. Petersburg

18. Clara **Hildegard** von Boetticher, daughter of I, 14; born September 12 (24), 1883, in Stolpen—Göda

19. **Catharina** Alexandra von Boetticher, sister of II, 16; born December 17 (29), 1885 (posthuma), in Stephanpol—Stephanpol

III. Married and Widowed Boetticher Daughters

1. **Caroline** Amalie, widow Kuehn (née von Boetticher), sister of I, 4 (was married—April 30 (May 12), 1842, to the pastor in Kruthen, later in Eckau, Alexander Eberhard **Ernst** Kuehn, born June 18 (30), 1814†, January 22 (February 3, 1856), born January 1 (13), 1822, in Riga †—Riga

2. Louise **Amalie**, widow von Pacht (née von Boetticher), sister of I, 4 (was married—September 6 (18), 1847, with the pastor in Kokenhusen and Kroppenhof, **Hermann** Georg Meinhard von Pacht, born April 25 (May 7), 1816†, September7 (19), 1880, born January 6 (18), 1823 in Riga—Riga

3. **Helene**, widow von Radetzky-Mikulicz (née von Boetticher), sister of I, 2 (was married—May 15 (27), 1846, with Royal Russian Councillor and State Councillor **Carl** Alexander von Radetzky-Mikulicz, born May 15 (27), 1821†, April14 (26), 1887, born September 21 (October 3), 1823, in Mitau—Leipzig

4. Clara **Mathilde** von Bidder (née von Boetticher), sister of I, 10 (married—February 24 (March 8), 1862—with the April 17 (29), 1826, born, Royal Russian Cavalry Captain Retired **Heinrich** von Bidder), born February 27 (March 11), 1837, in Mitau—Mitau

5. **Olga** Skolon (von Boetticher), daughter that on November 14 (26), 1849†, **Johann** Carl Ernst von Boetticher (married to the Cossack leader Skolon), born in 1846 in Irkutsk

6. **Elise** von Peretz (née von Boetticher), daughter that on December 20, 1847 (January 1, 1848) †, **Gustav** Ernst von Boetticher (married to the Royal Russian lieutenant general, leader of the Mountain Corps von Peretz), born in St. Petersburg—St. Petersburg

7. **Leontine** von Nabél (née von Boetticher), sister of III, 6 (married Royal Russian Lieutenant General and Divisions Commander von Nabél)

8. **Maria** Pabst, (née von Boetticher), daughter of I, 4 from the I marriage (married June 29 (July 11), 1875, to Mayor **Carl** August Pabst, born on July 11 (23), 1835), born September 24 (October 6), 1851, in Zschillchau—Weimar

9. **Elisa** Emilie Drachenhauer (née von Boetticher), sister of I, 15 (married December 12 (24), 1875, to the owner of Neurahden and Krussen, **Edward** Drachenhauer, born October 6 (18), 1842), born October 27 (8 November), 1852, in Pommusch—Riga

10. Wilhelmine **Emilie** von Krannhals (née von Boetticher), sister of I, 15 (married May 31 (June 12), 1881, with Judge and Council Advocate **Carl** von Krannhals, born April 7 (19), 1856), born July 28 (August 9), 1856, in Pommusch—Riga

11. **Eugenie** Curti (née von Boetticher), daughter of I, 4 from the first marriage (married September 9 (21), 1880, to Componisten **Franz** Curti, born November4 (16), 1854), born May 12 (24), 1858 in Dresden—Dresden

12. **Maria** Helene von Bilterling (née von Boetticher), sister of I, 15 (married, August 2 (14), 1885) to estate owner August von Bilterling, born February 7 (19), 1854), born January 9 (21), 1860, in Pommusch—Pankelhof

13. **Frieda** Kreysern (née von Boetticher), daughter of I, 4 from the second marriage (married March 29 (April 10), 1885, to Royal Prussian Staff Doctor Dr. Barthol. Friedr. Albert **Georg** Kreysern, born August 12 (24), 1858), born June 7 (19), 1862, in Dresden—Metz

14. **Helene** Mathilde Bergengruen (née von Boetticher), daughter of I, 5 (married November 9 (21), 1889, to Doctor of Medicine **Paul** Emil Bergengruen, born July 17 (29), 1861), born February 21 (March 5), 1862, in Grenzhof—Riga

15. **Elisabeth** Strojew (née von Boetticher), sister of I, 45 (married January 24 (February 5), 1864, to **Constantin** Strojew, a nobleman of the Twer government), born January 22 (February 3), 1849

16. **Anna** Popow (née von Boetticher), sister of I, 45 (married September 10 (22), 1880, to a nobleman of the Nowgorod government Popow), born January 20 (February 1), 1859

17. **Sophia** Wassiliew (née von Boetticher), sister of I, 45 (married April 8 (20), 1879, to the Royal Russian Ulan Lieutenant Ilja Wassiliew), born July 18 (30), 1861

IV. Boetticher Wives and Widows

1. **Thecla** Marie von Boetticher (née von Bidder), widow that on March 30 (April 11), 1855† of knights manor owner of Kuckschen **Johann** Christoph Ernst von Boetticher, and the daughter of _____ 1833† Courlandic Medical Inspector, Collegian Councillor and Knight Doctor of Medicine **Heinrich** von Bidder and the _____, 1839 † **Amalie**, née Keidel, born February 24 (March 8), 1812, in Mitau—Mitau

2. **Helene** von Boetticher, widowed Kriloff (née Korndorf), wife of I, 3 and the daughter of _____, born December 12 (24), 1819, in Tula—Riga

3. **Alexandra** von Boetticher (née von Friede), II wife of I, 4 and daughter that on October 11 (23), 1877†, Royal Russian Major General Ret. Carl Johann von Friede and the December 14 (26), 1826†, **Thecla** (née von Reichard), born May 14 (26), 1822, in Tuckum—Dresden

4. **Alexandra** Juliane von Boetticher (née von Sengbusch), wife of I, 6 and daughter of the October 12 (24), 1880†, Royal Swedish Counsel and Knight, owner of the firm Sengbusch Ltd. in Riga **Wilhelm** von Sengbusch and September 24 (October 6), 1856†, **Catharina** (née Lamprecht), born April 27 (May 9), 1835, in Riga—Spirgen

5. **Eliza** Catharina von Boetticher (née Thoms), wife of I, 7 and daughter of the March 6 (18), 1846†, owner of the export company Henry Thoms Company in Riga, **Henry** Thoms that on April 22 (May 4), 1870†, **Emilie** Sophie (née Nöltingk), married von Hollander, born July 31 (August 12), 1839, in Riga—Ebelshof

6. **Johanna** Marie Elisabeth von Boetticher (née von Hollander, II), wife of I, 8 and daughter that on March 6 (18), 1868† founder and director of the private high school in Birkenruh, Knight Dr. **Albert** von Hollander and the October 8 (20), 1882†, **Polly** Charlotte Dorothea Elisabeth (née Rathleff), born January 19 (31), 1844, in Birkenruh—Riga

7. **Anna** Charlotte von Boetticher (née Heisler), wife of I, 9 and daughter of the September 21 (October 3), 1870†, Marchand Daniel **Friedrich** Heisler that on November 23 (December 5), 1844† Mathilde Emma (née Almuss), born November 18 (30), 1844, in Gross—Glogau—Warschau

8. **Antonie** Marie Caroline von Boetticher (née Baroness von Behr), wife of I, 10 and daughter that on March 4 (16), 1886†, Baron **Alduin** Rudolph von Behr of Neu-Moken and **Elisabeth** (née Edlen von Rennenkampff), born May 23 (June 4), 1851, in Behrs–Würzau–Kuckschen

9. **Julie** von Boetticher (née von Tallberg), wife of I, 13 and daughter of the States Councillor **Ottomar** von Tallberg and **Julie** (née Diewel), born February 13 (25), 1856, in _____—Riga

10. **Annette** Caroline von Boetticher (née Pander), wife of I, 11 and daughter that on October 1 (13), 1874†, honourary citizen and estate owner **Robert** Theodor Pander and **Auguste** Jacobine (née Drachenhauer), born March 20 (April 1), 1857, in Libau—Riga

11. Agathe **Isabella** Victoria von Boetticher (née von Wippermann), wife of I, 14 and the daughter that on November 24 (December 6), 1863†, estate owner **Hermann** Anton von Wippermann and the July 23 (August 4), 1865†, Ann **Caroline** (née Boyes), born September 22 (October 4), 1859, in Davenport—Göda

12. **Anna** Elisabeth von Boetticher (née von Roques), widow of the September 10 (22), 1885†, knight manor owner of Stephanpol **Wilhelm** Carl Friedrich von Boetticher and daughter of the Royal Prussian Major Ret. **Hermann** von Roques that on May 20 (June 1), 1869†, **Wilhelmine** Dorothea (née von Sengbusch), born October 15 (27), 1859, in Cassel—Stephanpol

13. **Maria** Alexandrine von Boetticher (née San-Galli), wife of I, 12 and daughter of the Royal Russian States Councillor and Knight **Franz** San-Galli, Excellence and **Sophia** (née Rosinsky), born January 26 (February 7), 1862, in St. Petersburg—St. Petersburg

14. **Emily** Louise von Boetticher (née Deringer), wife of I, 15 and daughter that on January 2 (14), 1879†, drugstore owner and honourary citizen Friedrich Wilhelm **Eduard** Deringer and of **Emma** (née Hahr), born June 28 (July 10), 1864, in Riga—Pommusch

15. **Alexandra** von Boetticher (née Tarakanow), widow that on October 16 (28), 1875†, Royal Russian Staff Officer **Gustav** Friedrich von Boetticher and the daughter of the Nowgorod Nobleman Alexander Tarakanow, born March 22 (April 3), 1828, in Opotschka—Rshew

16. **Katharina** von Boetticher (née Kurow), wife of I, 45 and daughter of the Rjasan Nobleman Kurow, born _____

17. **Elisabeth** von Boetticher (née Trawin), wife of I, 47 and daughter of the Kostroma Nobleman Trawin, born _____

NEWS

about

the von Boetticher Family

Courlandic Branch

II. For the Year 1892

On Behalf of the Family Council

Edited by

Dr. Walter von Boetticher

Göda (Kingdom Saxony)

Manuscript printed in 50 copies

Bautzen
Printed by E. M. Monse
1892

Contents

Introduction

The family reunion of the year 1891, as usual, brought together many members of our family. They met in the hospitable house of Mayor Emil von Boetticher of Riga for serious discussions and a service of remembrance. At the meeting of the family council, it was decided to grant the amount of 100 rubles for the printing of the second edition of the family news. Before the festive meal, Emil spoke to the 30 family members about the importance of that day. Here are his words:

My dear guests!

I will drink from this silver pitcher that was given 52 years ago by 12 friends to my parents for their 25th wedding anniversary, as it is an old custom to welcome all of you to celebrate this November 1. This is not only a day of business to distribute the charity money of the council, but mainly a day of remembrance to remember all those who contributed during their lifetime to the legat, to help all descendants. May the old pitcher be passed around the table and, as you drink from it, may everyone be taken back to an old time!

In the meantime, allow me now to answer these questions: Whom do we celebrate and who is called to celebrate?

Just now, 77 years and 7 hours have passed since Emilie Constantia Wippert waited in her parents' house on Herren Street in Riga, dressed in her bridal grown to meet her groom, Heinrich Carl Johann Boetticher, who led her to the altar of the Petri Church at twelve o'clock noon on November 1, 1814. I don't know who else was there besides the father of the bride, her brother Michael Heinrich Wippert, the stepsisters Margaretha Jacobina Kyber (née Fock) and Anna Carolina Fock. What happened at the ceremony I don't know at this time but we know about poetic "field flowers," seeded by an admirer of the bride at the wedding and this muse was also widely used by the friends of the groom at a time when the protocol was less rigid than it is today in the form of wishes and hints for the newlyweds. The old father of the groom was not well enough to attend the wedding of his son in Riga and his, at the time, active wife, stayed home to look after him and the household in Goldingen. We would not have much information without the letters that Emilie Boetticher, as bride and then young wife, had written to her mother-in-law regularly, talking about her household and how she felt during the early years of her married life. Now, with these letters, it's possible for us to go back in time to the parents' house and the first love, a time of pure luck and highest bliss;

at the same time we experience the magic in every letter that brings out the personality of the author.

I want to point out that after days of great happiness with the high point being the birth of the first daughter, Emilie, there followed days of heavy suffering and sorrow. The old house on Scheunen Street, which the parents bought in 1815, could talk about many wounds felt by the parents after many children died who had been first so happy in this house. These wounds were not healed at the time of the Silver Anniversary in 1839. Three years before the parents had lost their firstborn, the lovely Emilie. She had just gotten married to Dr. Sommer. At the same time the youngest son was born and was named after her (Emil), but this did not compensate for the loss. Still, everyone celebrated, in part because of the children and some of the older ones in our midst may remember and you alone may be able to talk about these festivities. I just want to mention that at this time eight children celebrated with their parents. Now there are 85 living descendants of which 31 have the name Boetticher. The rest are: 10 Pacht; 9 Kuehn; 8 Kieseritzky; 6 Drachenhauer; 5 Helmsing; 5 Curti; 3 Bitterling; 3 Pabst; 3 Kreysern; 2 Krannhals. Of the 85 descendants, 49 are male and 36 are female. Eighteen are married, 2 are widowed, 1 is engaged and 64 are neither married nor engaged. Of the 49 living male descendants 6 are estate owners and farmers, 5 are lawyers, 4 are students, 3 are doctors, one is an author, one is a forester and 28 are still young. I am sure that all the descendants of our parents, who celebrated their wedding 77 years ago, will keep a fond memory of them. To keep this memory of the parents with all the many happenings and characters alive for the future generations, we have to in time, so nothing gets lost, document their life story. I am sure the publication of next year's second edition, which leads us back into the parents' house, everybody, who looked through the first edition with interest, wants to read.

May this wish be an incentive for everyone to contribute, especially those who have personal memories of stories that I do not possess. With the plea that the first edition is received well and the second one will be supported, I request that all present here today work with all the descendants of our parents so they will be kept in high esteem and remembered forever and ever!

The interest that the first edition of the family news received was not only proof of the general need for information about the family history; it also gives us a guarantee for its future blossoming and thriving. If a family or nation loses sight of its past or shows little interest in it, it is a sure sign of decline for the family and a political powerlessness and destruction.

The following second edition is dedicated in memory of Carl and Emilie von Boetticher. To paint us a picture of their work and striving throughout their lives in career, home and family; to keep this picture alive for the future generations; and to point out the significance for the family—these had been the tasks for Mayor Emil von Boetticher, who, with endless effort and lots of love, mastered this work. The family thanks him for the following.

VI. Generation

A. Councillor Heinrich Carl Johann von Boetticher (1782–1859) and His Family

Part I

From His Birth to His Silver Anniversary

Chapter 1

Birth, Education and Years as Apprentice

Heinrich **Carl** Johann von Boetticher was born in Goldingen on March 5, 1782, at 5:00 a.m. His birthday was a Sunday, but the life that followed brought mostly work and often worries. Those did leave in later years, when the time of endless energy had passed; he hated to grow older. Even so, Carl Boetticher deserved to be called a Sunday child. In his sensitivity and his quiet work habits, it was the peacefulness of a Sunday morning, and his friendly heart knew nothing about hostility and hatred. He liked to help others, and thankfully he seemed to forget easily and often. A wide circle of people loved him, and his name was always spoken with admiration.

For the baptism of this Sunday child, the father, Johann Friedrich Boetticher, the Honourable Mayor of the dukedom city of Goldingen, invited the honouraries of the town on March 9, 1782.

Carl Boetticher was brought up in his parents' house. There everything was kept simple, and they made efforts not to spoil the child. His father was a great example of diligence, and his mother loved him tenderly so that his good character developed nicely. His relationship to his parents, even though stiff in the old form of the 18th century, was loving and characterized by childlike submission.

For his education, he went to the city school in Goldingen. Carl had to leave school early to start his apprenticeship as a merchant. We do not know if this was his wish or if this was his father's idea. Later on in his life, he often regretted not having more education and the opportunities that the men in his surroundings had.

It is important to mention the political situation in his homeland during his younger years. In the last decades of the 18th century, the Dukedom of Courland experienced constant quarrels between the Duke and the nobility, and this led to the downfall of the country. The anarchistic Poland gave no support, everything was in disarray, and the cities fell apart. As expected, Russia annexed Courland in 1796, which brought great relief to the population, and everyone was thankful to the monarch and the descendants. Carl Boetticher had the same feeling towards the Russian Empire and its monarch and showed them great admiration and love. Under their steady leadership, the economy in his homeland would greatly improve in the years ahead.

Carl was still a boy when he was sent to Libau to apprentice as a commercial trader. At that time, Libau was not the "Wunder City" it is today, but the only commercial port in Courland. One could learn a great deal there, only this "school" was not easy. The apprentices had to work hard for their bosses in warehouses and shops and did many jobs that would be done today by regular workers. For the mayor's son, there was no exception. Carl was reliable and did his duty but regretted having little time to do any studying. When he was done with his *apprenticeship* for the strict Mr. Bäckmann, he looked for employment that would leave him more time for furthering his education. His goal was Riga. There he could count on good teachers and learn in his spare time.

Before he took this important step, Carl got in contact with his uncle Carl Friedrich von Boetticher in Mitau. This uncle looked after the children of his only brother, Mayor Boetticher, as if they were his own. He loved them, and his wealth provided for their advancement. As an experienced businessman, he had many friends in Riga, and they found employment for Carl at the commerce of Hülsen and Ruben. His salary was small, but this was not important. The uncle in Mitau wrote to Carl on September 15, 1805, "If I were your age, I would prefer Riga over Libau; you know Libau well and have also been to Riga, but Riga is a much different place. Do as you wish, I will not convince you, as it is your decision. If you are in Riga, beware of bad company, and you will be fine."

In October 1805, Carl Boetticher moved to Riga, his new hometown, as a stranger who could not count on any support from friends or family. However, he was sure if he stayed true to himself, success would follow. His work had God's blessing. His performance brought him acknowledgement, and his friendly character brought him new friends. For seven more years, he was employed. We don't know if he worked all that time for the same company.

Chapter 2

Starting His Own Company and Household, His Marriage

Carl Boetticher was now a man with knowledge and experience, trusted by many and with friendships among the best. With these attributes and the necessary money from his uncle in Mitau, he established his own company with his friend Eduard Wilhelm Lösevitz in the year 1812.

Carl did not see his commercial business as a game of luck but carefully checked the needs of the public and adjusted his operation accordingly. His profit came not by chance; he calculated but did not speculate.

His decision to start his business was not the best. The big war (1812 between France and Russia) slowed the traffic of goods down and the money lost buying power, but the young businessman was happy with a small margin of profit. In the next year, he became sick as rheumatism befell his body; his eyes too were affected. The strong pain did not let him sleep, and the constant fever took all his energy. Carl had to leave all work to his friend Lösevitz, but he never gave up hope. With the help of Dr. Redlich and the love of his friends, he was brought back to health. By October 1813, he was able to move freely again and return to work. In the meantime, the business went well, and he hoped that with the victory of the army over France and a peace agreement, new chances for his company would open up, too. In November 1813, he wrote his uncle that the first year had brought him a good income. He was happy in Riga with its many opportunities, and he would not move to any other place. It was also clear to him if he had the necessary funds, his company could be greatly expanded.

The more success Carl had, the more time he spent at his business. He loved the work, especially that it could give him the basis for the establishment of his own household.

Before he had become sick, he had met Emilie Wippert. They fell in love with each other. Emilie was 18 years old and, at that time, graceful and charming. She had a clear intellect and a good education in her parents' house and in part at Pastor Kuehn's house in Eckau, so that her talents were harmoniously developed. Her father loved her dearly and had given her a deeply religious influence without losing sight of the practical side of life. The engagement was a secret for now (Carl's wish). The newly established business had to be secured first. But it was not easy for Emilie to keep this secret, so the first person to get the news was Carl's uncle in Mitau.

Three months later, Carl and Emilie celebrated their wedding in front of the altar of the Petri Church in Riga on November 1, 1814, at noon. Carl's parents were not able to attend because his father was not well enough to make the trip at this time of year and his mother had to look after him. We don't know what relatives of the bride besides her father and her two stepsisters attended the ceremony. Nothing is known about the party afterwards.

Chapter 3

Emilie as Wife and Housewife, Birth of the First Child, Death of Carl Friedrich von Boetticher

The young couple worked hard. On January 23, 1815, Emilie writes:

> My husband works a lot; he gets up early in the morning and goes to bed late at night. I, on the other hand, have some free time during the day. I love my house very much and hate to leave it even and do my chores to my heart's content. My friends wonder why I spend so much time behind my four walls.

On August 7, 1815, their first child, a girl, was born, and in October 1815, she was baptized in the Petri Church. Carl had hoped that his parents could attend, but they did not leave Goldingen. The child received the name of her grandmother Marie and also her mother, Emilie.

A few months before the birth of the child, Carl's uncle, Carl Friedrich von Boetticher, who had been sick for a while, had died. This uncle had always been good to him, and Carl mourned deeply. The deceased left a large estate, but the will had not been completed. According to the law, his brother, Mayor Johann Friedrich

Boetticher, got all the assets. The old mayor now had the money to leave Goldingen, but it took two more years before he could sell his houses and get everything arranged in the town of his lifelong activity before he moved to Riga.

Chapter 4

Carl's Siblings, His Business Life, Purchase of the House on Scheunen Street, Thorensberg

Since Carl's wedding, his sister Amalie had also lived in Riga. She was 14 years old when she moved into his house to attend the schools and private classes in town. Carl's younger brother Johann studied first in Dorpat and later at universities in Germany. His other brother (the youngest) first worked in Riga and then in England and France to become a merchant. All the children of Carl's parents had left home. Amalie was a happy-go-lucky child, helping her sister-in-law with the household and the little girl, whom she carried through the house singing songs to her. In the meantime, her schoolwork was lacking. The teacher, Grass, taught Dorothea Lösevitz, a sister of Edward W. Lösevitz's and Amalie at home. "Dorchen" lived now in Carl's house also and so the family grew quickly. For lunch, Dorchen's brother, Carl's friend and business partner, was always invited. Over time, Edward Lösevitz and Amalie fell in love and got married in the year 1820.

It is easy to see that the rooms Carl lived in soon were too small for his family, so he began looking for a large house of his own with space for the household and his business. In September 1815, he bought the house on Scheunen Street in Riga and moved there in 1816.

This house, previously owned by Mr. Sommer, was at that time one of the best established in the city. On October 9, 1815, Emilie wrote,

> I checked out our new house and find it very comfortable. Here I can do all my housework without going outside into the cold. The English kitchen keeps the house warm and has a pump and a sink (which is very rare here). Everything is nice and we look forward to living here. In January we will move into our house and I have to order and arrange many things. I would really like to get some advice from my good mother on how to organize the rooms.

In the meantime, Carl was very successful with his business at this new location, and his hard work paid off well. The first daughter grew up nicely, and her parents were happy and proud. Many other children followed. The circle of friends grew steadily. Everyone loved the hospitality of the host and hostess and their friendly and cheerful ways. Many festivities took place in the Boetticher house. It was not a place of pomp or splendor but was cozy and comfortable. Whenever someone needed help of any kind, Carl looked after it.

Not only days of good luck, but also many of sorrows entered the Boetticher house. There the parents mourned the deaths of nine of 17 children and especially the death of their oldest daughter, Marie Emelie, the wife of Dr. Friedrich Sommer. She was in the prime of her life. Later on, Carl Boetticher's life was often filled with grief. His wife had died, and all the empty rooms gave him great sadness.

The Boettichers lived on the third floor of the house. The business occupied the first floor, and on the second floor, Carl had an apartment built for his parents. It took all of Carl's and Emilie's powers to convince the parents to move. Carl wrote, "Don't you want to see your grandchild? She is a lovely and lively child. We will do everything to make your life in old age as comfortable as possible." In the spring of 1816, his parents moved from Goldingen into the apartment on the second floor.

Carl took no holidays and was working very hard, 15 hours daily with little rest. His young wife was busy with her household and child but felt she needed more out of life. She longed to get more education, to know more about nature and the arts. She wanted to travel, see the world, and learn about new things. When news arrived from her brothers-in-law that they were traveling the world, she too felt the longing to travel and see places outside of Riga. She wrote, "Even though I am very happy with my fate, when I read the letters of Gustaf, I wish I was a man to travel the world, but a woman's life is in her house and that's where I will be."

The longing to get away from the confined barriers of the household did not diminish her joy and happiness at home and with her child. In March 1816, she wrote,

Never before have I looked more forward to the warmer time of the year, to take the little one outside into the fresh air. Sunday we walked to our new summer residence. The trees had no sign of any leaves, but the grass showed the first sign of green and our hearts were happy. What a nice life we will have once we have moved into the country!

It was a modest place where Carl and Emilie spent their summer months. It was near the Marien Mill on Thorensberg. Mr. Weiss had a factory with a house and garden. There they rented some rooms for the summer with fresh air and the songs of the birds. They were happy days with old Mr. Weiss, and Carl and Emilie had fond memories of that place, even after they had purchased the beautiful Ebelshof.

Chapter 5

Birth and Death of the Second Child, Emilie's Letters

Carl and Emilie went back early in the fall of 1816 to their house in the city. On September 10, their second daughter was born, and on October 1, she was baptized with the name of Anna Constantia. Three days later, the little one died. We find nothing in any letters about the deep pain that Emilie must have felt. Certainly this was not an easy time, but life had to go on. When Carl had to travel to St. Petersburg on business a few months later, Emilie left her daughter with her mother-in-law and travelled with him. For a few weeks, she really enjoyed her stay in this magnificent residence city.

Emilie wrote two letters from St. Petersburg to Riga, and these are the last ones of her younger years that survived. Between 1817 and 1840, we have no letters from her, but there are many from the last 15 years of her life. This large number of letters gives us a pretty good picture of her complete life. The years between 1817 and 1840 are the busiest for Carl and a time of great joy and great sorrow for him and his wife. It is too bad we do not have any information about what they experienced during this time. But with the letters to her mother-in-law in Riga, we will now relive the trip to St. Petersburg.

Petersburg, January 22, 1817,

Eight days ago we were still very close to Riga and our thoughts were often with you. The road was actually pretty nice, except for some wet areas; we went at a gallop to the first station. Carl asked me: Are we really going to Petersburg? Yes, I answered but was a bit worried about the river Aa, because people said it is still open. To turn back now, so far from Riga, was not a pleasant thought. Our trip was done with good humor. Even though we had to exchange our wagon with an ordinary smaller one in Dorpat, where Carl had some problems with it, he was always happy. Mr. Wagner was nice enough to take us on a moonlit trip through Dorpat. It looks like a friendly place especially nice in the summer. On our return trip we plan to visit here for a day to see the important sights. Please write to me, dear Mother, about housekeeping concerns, so that I at least keep these things on my mind with all that goes on here. How is our father and how is my dear sweet child, my Milie? If she were here, I would be even happier. I wrote a long letter to Dorchen and Malchen and they will probably tell you about it. We have to see a lot more and I wish we will not be invited often, to have more time.

Petersburg, January 29, 1817

Every hour I think of you, dear Mother, and all things about Riga are so very close to my heart. Even when I look at all the beautiful splendor and human art and skill, my thoughts are with my lovely house and its occupants and I wish I could share this pleasure with you. On January 27 we got mail, which I enjoyed a lot because it is very important for me to know what is happening at home if I want to have fun at our stay in Petersburg. The people we have got to know here try very hard to show us a good time. We have seen the Hermitage Art Museum, a glass factory, a porcelain factory, a cotton factory, an arsenal, a mint, a wallpaper factory, Taurish Palais, and other nice things, among them some beautiful ballet. In short, Mother, you would not recognize us with all this revelry. Carl, who works so very hard when he is at home in his business, is now restless and asks when we are in our quarter for an hour, what can we do now? If we have a new idea, we take our fur coats and Iswoschtschik, the coachman, will drive us to a new place. This evening we had tea at Kresnoi Kabak and enjoyed the famous waffles. Tomorrow morning we will make the trip to the Tsar's summer residence

Zarskje Selo. This is pretty far and we'll be back later this evening.

I hope, my dear Mother, the household gives you not too much trouble and you are not mad at your daughter who has it so nice. When I come back home I will try to get quickly back into the old routine. If you find the time, please write a few lines. With this great distance, news from our Riga is very much appreciated, especially when it comes from my dear people. To my child a hundred kisses. Oh, how I would like to give them this moment myself! To all others I send greetings from your respectful daughter, Emilie.

Chapter 6

Sorrow and Good Times in the Family, Trip to Germany, Mayor Carl Schwabe in Weimar, Seventh Wedding Anniversary

Emilie had greatly enjoyed her first trip, but being away from home showed her how strong the connection to Riga was. She loved coming home to look after her household and her little darling daughter.

On October 25, 1817, a son was born. He received the name Carl Friedrich after his dead uncle, but he died on November 19, 1817. Carl suffered from catarrh and rheumatism, which gave them much concern. In the summer of 1818, he needed spa treatments in a foreign country. The result was good, but Carl's father was very sick by then. He died on May 10, 1819, after a long illness. The same year, on October 12, another son was born. He was given the name of his grandfather Johann. A year after the grandfather died, this child was also dead on May 18, 1820. A child born on October 17, 1820, died after only two days. This was a difficult time for the parents, but they never lost courage. Carl worked hard to ease the pain, and Emilie felt solace and thanked God that her oldest daughter was alive and well.

During this time of great sorrows in the life of the Boetticher parents was the happy occasion of Amalie's engagement to Edward

Wilhelm Lösevitz. The old father had given his blessings before he passed away. One year later, on May 2, 1820, the wedding was celebrated in Carl's house. The same day, the sister of the young husband, Dorothea Lösevitz, got engaged to Mr. Friedrich Rosenkranz, and this gave them reason for special celebrations. Many guests attended.

In the year 1821, the Boetticher couple made a trip to Germany. The goal was to get some spa treatments, which Emilie especially needed, but it brought many pleasures also. The trip to Thüringen and onto the River Lahn near Spa Ems and the art treasures of Berlin and Dresden made deep impressions on Emilie.

In different towns, they made new and lasting friendships. The Sasse family in Berlin, the vom Berges in Remscheid, and especially the Schwabes in Weimar became close friends of the Boettichers in Riga. Mayor Carl Schwabe and his wife, Louise, really took a liking to the "excellent Boetticher and his great wife." This is clearly shown in the letters between Riga and Weimar, when the friends exchanged their thoughts over the long distance. In a letter from the year 1825, Schwabe writes to his friend how happy he is to hear about the success of the Spa Ems, the problems in his office, and the joys of his family life. He also talks about a gift Carl Boetticher had sent him. He wrote,

The small box that you gave me, I use all the time and God willing as long as I live. The other 24 boxes which I own, are now in "pension" for good; the C. B. on this box that I like so much, not only stands for Carl Boetticher, no, it means also: "carus, ja carissimus Boetticher, and so it shall be forever!"

And so it was on until the last hours of this true friend. He died eight years before Carl Boetticher. He was a giving person who received much love during his life.

Ems (a famous spa city) the actual destination of the trip, with its wells and baths, had worked well. The travellers got back in the fall of 1821 to Riga, physically stronger and mentally refreshed. There their friends had missed them dearly. All this was a good opportunity to celebrate the seventh wedding anniversary of the Boetticher couple. The obligatory poem was printed on a pink ribbon for this occasion to help them remember this beautiful day.

Carl Boetticher was a stranger when he moved to Riga. But long before he established his own household, he felt at home. His honourable character brought him many friends, who belonged to the larger family circle. They shared the good and the bad times together, and it was not empty convenience but a deeper feeling towards everyone. The hospitality of the Boetticher house left a lasting impression on all guests and friends.

Chapter 7

At the Height of His Power, Purchase of the Estates Plahnen and Klingenberg, Election as Councillor, Carl's Charitable Work

With the seventh wedding anniversary, a new chapter began for Carl and Emilie Boetticher. At that time, they only had one daughter, Marie Emilie. By the time their silver anniversary came around, 18 years later, the oldest daughter had died, but five sons and three daughters celebrated with their parents. The children lived for 42 more years before the first one of them died. In the first seven years of their parents' marriage, five children were born and four passed away. In the following 18 years, another 12 children saw the light of the world, but four died early. It seemed the number of eight should not be exceeded, because when the youngest arrived (number 17), the oldest closed her eyes forever. Even though there were heavy losses in this part of their life, especially the passing of Emilie, the suffering was not as great as in former years. Life became more peaceful, and even after bad times, good luck and success came back.

At this time, Carl Boetticher was at the height of his power and productivity. The physical suffering of his earlier years (rheumatism and catarrh) had left him, he had gained some weight, and he looked good. Pictures show a finely formed, slightly bent nose and friendly eyes, which emitted cheerfulness and goodwill. Carl still looked after his business with great care, but he had more time now compared to previous times when he said, "I have no time for enjoyment, nor can I think of diversion. There is just no time to think about it." Even though the partnership with Lösevitz had ended during the early 1820's (Lösevitz started his own business) and Carl was now the sole owner of his establishment, he found ample time for other things, including time to receive guests in his house.

After his father, Carl Friedrich von Boetticher, died, Carl received part of his estate. It took years of negotiations, which Carl was already leading when his parents were still alive, and he did so also for his siblings. A part of the inheritance consisted of the Estate Plahnen, which Carl's brother Gustav took over (transaction May 4, 1821), and after his death (1828), Carl and his brother Johann became the owners (transaction September 21, 1829). Two years later, Carl was the sole owner (transaction November 30, 1831), and this business took much of his time. At this time, he purchased the Estate Klingenberg in Livland (a province in Latvia), and this too needed his attention. Furthermore, he was the business manager for his brother Johann, who had bought the Estate Kukschen in Courland, for his brother Gustav, owner of Eckengraf. After Gustav's death, he managed it too for the widow. Carl also looked after other relatives and their business adventures. For them, he organized the selling of the products from the estates. He made purchases, invested their money, and gave out credits. The brothers in the country, the cousins in the military, and the aunts who did not live in Riga all went to Carl when they were in the city and needed anything, knowing he would do his best to help.

A man with such energy and willingness to be there for others soon found the attention of the Riga communal services. By a mutual vote of the council of the Great Guild, Carl was appointed a member on October 3, 1827, and on October 5, 1827, he was voted into the Riga City Council. He was sworn in with the newly appointed gentlemen Friedrich Germann, Gustaf Schlichting, Carl Holst, and Bernhard Christian Grimm. He was an assessor at the court in the Department of Agriculture and also a delegate of the Office for Business and Alcohol Tax Commission. These appointments took a lot of his time but left him very unsatisfied. As an assessor at this court, he had no say in the outcome of the verdict. His superior did this. Spending wasteful hours three times a week was not for him. So after his two-year term was up, he resigned. The council tried to convince him otherwise but without success, and on September 15, 1829, Carl left his office.

Even though he was no longer a member of the council board, he was known everywhere as Councillor Boetticher, and after he had resigned his position, he spent many hours working for the common good of other people. He dedicated his time as guardian, advisor and representative for widows. He organized the estates of the surviving dependents with great skill and energy and was reliable and successful. He worked until late at night to organize the paperwork of people who had passed away and in this way made sure the dependents' future was secure. Often Carl Boetticher gave freely where it was needed the most. At times, he took orphans into his house. Rosalie Alberti and her brother and Minna Lindenberg found their second home there and were thankful to Carl and his wife. Both felt the need to help others in great part out of religious reasons.

Chapter 8

Children of the Boettichers, Character Traits of Carl and Emilie

Carl's wealth and prestige grew, and his influence brought great results. His household changed and also grew. In the years between 1822 and 1828, one child was born every year, and during the years of 1830, 1831, 1833, 1835 and 1836, the family grew with a new baby every year.

Here is the complete register of all the children born during those years. We have also added the firstborn daughter, Emilie.

1.	Marie Emilie	born	August 7, 1815
2.–5.	children died young		
6.	Caroline Amalie	born	January 1, 1822
7.	Louise Amalie	born	January 6, 1823
8.	Carl Gustav	born	February 28, 1824
9.	Mathilde Jacobine Henriette	born	April 7, 1825
10.	Friedrich Heinrich	born	June 11, 1826
11.	Wilhelmine Auguste	born	August 14, 1827
12.	Gustav Leopold	born	September 16, 1828
13.	Theodor Philipp	born	April 7, 1830
14.	Elise Helene	born	September 2, 1831
15.	Johanna Auguste	born	June 24, 1833
16.	Carl Oscar	born	August 23, 1835
17.	Emil Friedrich	born	October 1, 1836

Being blessed with many children not only brought responsibilities but also happiness. Only the children who had lived there 60 years ago can talk about how happy their parents had been.

Carl Boetticher never spoke of his inner feelings. Bishop Dr. P. A. Poelchau at one time said, "He is not a man of many words, but a man of action."

One of Carl's daughters wrote,

I don't know if the years of our youth were different from other children, but I do know that we could always count on the love of our parents. In the mornings we all waited for our father to enter the room and every one of us wanted to be first to kiss and receive a friendly word from him. After he sat down for his morning coffee, we crowded around, the smaller ones climbing onto the chairs, to get a teaspoon full of coffee, before he started his breakfast. Then we brought the big tobacco box and his favorite long pipe with the porcelain head. During the daytime, Father was busy but in the evening he took the smallest child in his arms while the others held onto him. Mother played the piano and with great jubilation we all ran through the house. Father loved his children dearly and cared for them. For hours during the day and at night he carried the sick little Mathilde in his arms when the child did not find comfort in her bed. Even though most of the care and the upbringing of the children was done by our mother, Father loved every progress that we made, but he would be quite critical if he disliked anything and we all had to pay attention. If we needed anything, he gave us what we had asked for and at that time reminded us to be frugal. Of course, he liked it when we thanked him, but this was not that important to him. He often helped in secrecy and was happy if his surprises had worked. I don't think we were spoiled, but we learned to enjoy the little things, which others overlooked. We had great fun when the first snowflakes fell and the sparrows sat in the eaves, or we saw the baker apprentice near the window at the bakery Knaak covered in flour, or when Mrs. Dussing in the neighbor's house fed the canary, the cat and the dog from the same dish, or when we talked with our "Papchen," our old gray parrot (a friend of the young and the old). Our mother taught us the first children's songs with her lovely voice. She also taught us to read, to count the days and the months and more. I often wished to be the sole owner of an apple or an orange, but in our house it was always: "Sharing, children, sharing!" and later on when this child's wish came true, I had no desire to do so unless I could share with someone.

Carl and Emilie Boetticher taught their children to be frugal and not to get used to luxury. They did not allow their boys and girls to wear better clothing or jewelry than the children of poorer parents. Unnecessary things were not allowed, and all the rest was supplied, especially if it helped to widen the horizons of the children. Any amount of money was spent for lessons, books and materials. Money to help with the education of the children was money well spent, and they would benefit more from it than any other investment. Their father encouraged not only his children to be moneywise but all other people who depended on him. Teachers, housemaids, servants—all of them were advised to save part of their income in a bank account with interest, and nobody ever left the household after a longer time period without taking some money along, which made them very thankful towards their advisor later on in life.

Carl Boetticher taught his children to be polite towards everyone. His daughter wrote:

When I had finished my piano exercises in the last room where the instrument stood in Ebelshof, and I was running out, I saw Father and Land Commissioner H. in the corner room talking. I bowed quickly in my haste, but our father called me back and said: "Did you not recognize Mr. H?" I understood the hint and made a really deep bow. Later on Father lectured me about the impoliteness and how embarrassed he had been. From then on I did not like Land Commissioner H. and rather climbed out the window one time to avoid bowing for him.

When it came to hard work, unpretentiousness and saving money, the parents provided a good example. Carl made sure to be courteous to everyone. His wife was always busy making things for the large family. As she worked, she hummed melodies that her children years later often recognized.

Carl was now in the position to afford the good things in life, while others around him had less. But that lifestyle was not for him and his wife, too, could have had an easier life. He continuously helped others and she did charitable work.

He was courteous to everyone. When he walked the city streets, everybody knew and greeted Councillor Boetticher and he would tip his hat even on cold days, returning the greeting. Carl appreciated the importance of work and honoured the tradesman, especially the chimney sweeps. "We have to be thankful towards them." After their work was done, they received a good meal in the kitchen and were rewarded on New Year's Day.

Carl was generous with his time and money and loved to help out. His wife did the same, often in the poorer neighborhoods of Riga and in the *Seifenbergen* further away. There she gave the people food, medicine, clothing, money and, of course, good advice. She loved to do this in her quiet way, and many worshiped her for this work. This was apparent especially after she had died and a lot of poor folks showed up at her gravesite to show their benefactor their last respects.

From his own experience, Carl knew that success is hard to come by if one does not have the necessary funds. In such cases, he helped the young entrepreneur and made sure that the finances he supplied were used correctly and wisely. He was very generous if he was convinced about the person. Students and others who started a new business life thanked him later after they were successful. If Carl trusted someone, he would support the person even though things did not always work out. The following is known.

A Mr. Jarre owned a sugar factory near Riga, and Carl Boetticher had supported him with some money. But the competition of the large Brandenburg sugar factories was too much and Jarre had money problems. All the worries and excitement had made him sick, and when Carl went to visit him, the scared man raised his hands and exclaimed, "I know why you're here, Councilman."

"No, Mr. Jarre," was the answer, "you don't know; and don't worry, I am here to help you, because this misfortune is not your fault and you are an honourable man."

But the new business went under and Carl Boetticher lost 30,000 rubles. He never blamed the owner and later on helped his family survive.

A young man with a mediocre job wanted financial support from Carl so he could marry his Marie, the maid who ran his household. Carl told him, "Young man, you cannot live on love. Work hard, get a well-paying job, and when you are successful come back and we will talk further."

His charity work must have been known far and wide because his daughter Amalie reports:

One day I drove to Friedrichstadt, years after our father had died. I drove my horses and wagon into the entrance at old Marcus Kahn's house to get some information in his little store. As soon as the old man had found out that I am the Pastor's wife from Kokenhusen, he happily exclaimed: "Amalie Pacht, Councillor Boetticher's daughter!" And then he ran into the house and with the help of his old wife dragged out a big chair into the small room and I had to sit down whether I wanted to or not. He then asked me a thousand questions: "How is Lina, the one that married Pastor Kühn, and how many children has she? How is Carl, the owner of Pommusch? Is he happy with his children? And Theodor and

Friedrich?" And many more. By that time, the small room had filled with men, women and children. "Look, look, this is the daughter of Councillor Boetticher the old Kahn said and then explained: "I was a poor Jew and wanted to earn some money, but could not get ahead. So I thought I will go to Councillor Boetticher as he had helped many. Maybe he would help me too. And so I went to him and he gave me 2,000 rubles. God had blessed me! But I paid everything back to the last penny. And one time, Mr. Councillor von Eckengraf came to me asking for money. I gave him what he had asked for and he paid me back to the last cent." Then Marcus Kahn introduced me to his daughters, sons-in-law and grandchildren. When I asked him about his sons, he became very earnest and replied: "I only had one, but he died."

Now I was supposed to stay and have a meal with them but this was a bit too much, as I had no more time. As I wanted to leave I was told: "We have nice papers, teas, materials and fine soaps and more. Just to make a good impression, I bought kerchiefs for the maids and knives for the servants."

Chapter 9

Friends, Purchase of Ebelshof, Life in General

Carl and Emilie Boetticher loved to entertain, and both were very good hosts. Mother liked the easy exchange of thoughts, and Father loved to share his comfortable house with friends. Both enjoyed having other young children in their house. This would make for more fun for the young and the old. Carl put great emphasis on morality, and Emilie was quite religious.

Many respectable men and lovely women were guests in the Boetticher house. Most of Carl's friends were merchants, and the following are some of their names: Thilo, Holm, Kyber, Dressler, Thonn, Bergengruen, Wittkowsky-Querfeldt, Lösevitz, Strauss, Westberg, Holst and Hernmarck. Many scholars were also close to the Boettichers, namely Pastor G. Bergmann, Mayor Kühn, Pastor Kröger, Dr. Hartmann, Dr. Bornhaupt, Superintendent Poelchau, Pastor Taube and Otto Müller. As the sons and daughters grew up, their friends came to visit at their parents' house to dance and play, to go for drives and to experience musical entertainment. On Sundays at dinner, the table was almost always extended to accommodate the many guests who spent lovely hours talking and joking. During these happy times, political questions had no importance. The conversations were about spiritual ideas and moral questions. The emphasis was on not material enjoyment but exchange of perceptions.

The best, nicest festivities were held at Ebelshof. Carl and Emilie Boetticher had spent the summer months at the Weiss Farm, but over time, this place got too crowded. They wanted their own gardens and summer residence. Carl loved the hobby of farming and looked for a property near Riga large enough for him to do so. He was happy to purchase Ebelshof from Count Dimitri Alexandrowitsch Subow, who lived in Petersburg and had no time to farm. The sales contract was signed with his representative Mr. von Rehbinder in May 1830. The same year, the Boetticher family moved to Ebelshof and from then on lived there during the months of May to October.

A citizen of Riga, Mr. Ebel, who gave this place his name, had owned this charming country estate during the previous decades. There he drained the land and built the park and gardens. It took many years before the trees and bushes were large enough to be planted singly or in groups near meadows, ponds and artificial hills to create a beautiful landscape. Mature pine forests, which gave this estate a special appeal, surrounded the fields, and it was easy to forget how close the city was (five kilometres?). When the Boettichers bought Ebelshof, it was still in its younger stages. The park had a romantic aura brought on by the grottos and temples and many shady hidden places to rest with clean gravel roads in between. Every mood was taken care of. There were spots to hide from the world or walk into the forest. All hearts opened on a quiet Sunday morning with the birds singing and the sounds of Riga's cathedrals ringing.

The large gardens produced plenty for the kitchen and cellar. In the hothouses, plants were raised for the flowerbeds and to decorate the rooms. The farm was well organized and large enough to support 30 milking cows and a creamery. In the evening, the cows came back from the fields with their bells ringing, and with the clouds above, the children felt transplanted into the faraway Alps.

A spacious house was at the entrance of the park. It had many guestrooms and was built so that one side got the cool shadow and the other had a wide deck looking out over a sunny open place surrounded by beautiful groups of trees. In the morning and evening light, the view from the deck was breathtaking. Carl Boetticher lived with his family in the main house. Close family members occupied two smaller houses in the park.

At Ebelshof, the younger people found everything that their hearts desired. For the parents, it also brought work for the upkeep and maintenance of this summer residence.

Carl was a friend of nature and at the same time a passionate farmer. He enjoyed every tree and shrub. He planted, took care of, removed and replaced them. He got advice from men of the trade and followed his own impulses. Existing grounds were enlarged and beautified and new ones created. Rare trees and shrubs were sent from far away and found a place in Ebelshof. Magnificent needle trees had to compete with the "venerable pine trees near the foot of the small temple hill." Almond bushes and walnut trees made the company of lilacs and American maples. Gardener Barlow's skilled hands had to resolve new tasks, and he was happy when he received a smile of approval from his boss.

Carl Boetticher took even greater care of his fields and the swamp nearby. It took many decades to convert this high swamp (and a lot of money and effort) into rich fields. He called this area his "new grounds." They were close to his heart, like a sick child that had to be loved and taken care of.

Every spring he was in a hurry to move from Riga to Ebelshof, and only the colder temperatures made him move back to the city. After his daily work was done in Riga, he quickly drove to Ebelshof during the spring and summertime to look after his farm and to enjoy the park. There he checked if the work was done according to his instructions. He gave new ones, and workers had to be paid and some had to be hired. As soon as this was done, he rode his horse out to the far places where work was completed but most often to his "new grounds." It was at this time he was happiest if one of his sons escorted him. Afterwards he enjoyed the park or the large deck. He checked on trees and plants, and it made him very happy if strangers (who had access to the park also) made comments about the beautiful grounds.

His wife shared the love of nature with him but also the passion for the farm. An important part of it was the creamery.

For a busy housewife, the creamery took a lot of her time. With the help of Mrs. Strauss, Emilie looked after the estate's milk production, which was quite substantial, and she also did the daily bookkeeping. After the money was counted and the amounts entered, the rubles were kept in a metal container to be used for Emilie's household expenses.

The fruit and vegetable gardens were also Emilie's responsibility. They produced plenty in the summertime, but it was time-consuming to prepare everything for the winter provision. It took a lot to feed the large family, the servants and the guests who sat at the hospitable Boetticher table.

With all the work in her house, gardens and cellars, Mother still found the time to go for walks. Even then her hands were busy knitting or cutting here and there with the large garden knife to make space among plants. On these occasions, Emilie would sing, competing with the birds in the dense branches, surrounded by the smell of the flowers in the spring air, thankful to the Giver of all Good, to whom she felt close. Sitting in hidden arbors reading was not for her. She walked out to a bench in the meadow; from there, she could see far, and she felt happy and content.

This lovely Ebelshof brought happiness to young and old and all the others who were invited.

Here the song of the nightingales mixed with those of the young girls. Here the boys felt the power of youth and all met on the lawns. On the evening walks to the Sandbergen or the "new grounds," everybody took part, and afterwards they all met on the steps of the big house to sing and joke into the night. During the haying season, the boys helped raking, but it was more fun to go into the barn and jump from high up into the soft hay below. The child carriage in the postal train through the large park, the boat on the pond, the horses in the barn or even better under the saddle, the family carriage ready for a trip—all these were wonderful attractions for the youth of the house who always had friends over in the summertime.

Like the young, the older generation always had friends and guests at this attractive place. In some papers of one of Carl Boetticher's daughters, we read about the time at Ebelshof.

Not only old friends showed up here at summertime, often for weeks, but also the pensioner teacher Buchholz, or the old Bergner (music teacher, organist) came over on Sunday afternoons as welcome guests. After the school day had ended, the boys found a lot of space for their games. Many years later I got a friendly letter form Leo von Engelhardt who called Ebelshof "The El Dorado of his youth." Many happy games were played and one day at the storming across the bridge to the small pavilion the stone bridge collapsed. At the end of this lovely day, Mr. Berner played the best children's songs and everybody sang along.

But for us, as our "life sun" is setting, Ebelshof still glows in the morning sun, when we think of our blissful days of youth in our El Dorado at the side of our parents.

Chapter 10

Hard Times, Twenty-Fifth Wedding
Anniversary, Carl Boetticher's Family Legat

It is not an easy task for me, the writer of this report (Emil Boetticher), to talk about the memories of this childhood and the early years. The inner eye sees the picture and endless melancholy surrounds us, yet we can only report in plain words. These appear sober and empty towards the real story. That is why the memories of all persons who lived through the good times should be used to fill in the blanks. The later generation must take in the whole picture of these golden pasts but also read between the lines.

Was the life in the Boetticher house in Riga and Ebelshof really just jubilation and good times? Did the children not see the tears in the eyes of their mother, which clearly showed her suffering? Those dark times have lost their sting now for those who lived through these times, and what is left are friendly pictures and the memories of happy days. Still we have to put some shade into this picture of the past.

In the time from 1821 to 1839, Carl and Emilie lost five children. The poor, weakly Mathildchen, who had cost her parents much heartache, lived only a few years. Auguste (born 1827) died young after failed efforts by the doctors. Gustav Leopold (born 1828) died young also, and so did Johanna Auguste (born 1833). Not only the deaths of the children worried the parents, but also their often-prolonged sicknesses. Amalie suffered from a food ailment that could be corrected by today's surgical standards with operations. But at that time it took long, painful spa treatments. The well-known Professor Dr. P. Walter did this in Wolmar. So Amalie, as a child, had to leave her parents' house and move to Wolmar where she lived with her future parents-in-law. The greatest loss for the parents was the death of their oldest daughter, the very talented and lovely Emilie. Everybody who knew her loved her. She died in the best years of her life and brought great heartache to all. She had just celebrated her 21st birthday (October 11, 1836) and was married two months before her death to the well-known Dr. Friedrich Sommer in Riga in May 22, 1836. Heartbroken over the loss of his wife, Sommer died half a year later. Her handwritten letters show her great personality, and her lively spirit is shown in the journal she wrote during the trip with her father in 1834 when she was only 19 years old as they visited natural and artistic treasures in Germany, Austria and Switzerland.

There is no need to describe the long grieving period of the parents. "God made us lose a lot, but he also gave us the power to overcome our losses," wrote our father many years later in memory of earlier times, and Mother too took the helping hand from above.

Three years had passed since Carl and Emilie Boetticher had lost their last child. During this time, they often visited the graves of their loved ones with flowers, supported by their many children. The day of the 25th wedding anniversary was near, and friends and children were prepared for this important occasion. Everybody competed for new surprises. The old Bergner composed festive music, and Superintendent Bergmann looked to entertain with happy and lighter music. Old and young, everybody had to contribute, to say something special to the silver anniversary couple, in poem form, in a serious or happy tone, and cheerfully to show them how much they were loved and revered and to wish them all the best from the people and from God. It was a festivity in a grand style at which eight children between the ages of three and 17 took part at the sides of their happy parents. Many guests from far away took part in the celebration on November 1, 1839, in the festive rooms of the Boetticher house. Many fantastic people now surrounded the celebrating couple. Many beautiful songs and friendly words were brought forward. In this atmosphere and with the love they had received, this day had to be commemorated. With his eight children and the future generations in mind, Carl Boetticher established a foundation on November 1, 1839.

"With the wish to help his descendants financially in case of any unforeseen problems they may have, Carl Boetticher provided 10,000 rubles (silver) on this date for a family legat." At this time, the capital in this legat is more than 75,000 rubles, and over many years different people have benefitted from the generous foundation. His descendants, which, at this time, are 80 people, will never forget the importance of the day November 1.

The first chapter in the life of the Boetticher couple ends with the date of November 1, 1839. After many years of hard work, it was now time to enjoy the fruits of their labor. Up to this point, all their energy went into establishing their own household, but now the future of the children was of great importance. They, too, must be helped to become successful in life. As the energy of the older generation diminishes, one is happy to watch the younger generation develop. After the best years of life, we all will get older very slowly. This transition into the third and last chapter of life we will now write about.

Part II

Trip Reports from the Years 1840 and 1841

Of the trip that my parents undertook with most of their children half a century ago, I, the youngest son and author, have only small recollections. I was just too young to grasp all the happenings. Therefore I would not be able to write a true report if it were not for the letters I found that my mother had written during that trip. A lively picture appeared in front of my eyes. Not only did I find my name, but through my mother's letters, I was able to see deeper into her rich heart and the way she saw all the beauty in life.

With this view in mind, I made the decision to write about these trips using her letters and add them to the *News about the von Boetticher Family*. My older siblings will have to forgive me if my report is not always correct or complete about the things that were said, heard, or experienced. It was of great importance to me to show from her letters how unforgettably Mother with her clear mind saw the outside world.

Chapter 1

From Riga to Kreuznach

On May 12, 1840, two large travel wagons were parked in front of the Boetticher house on Scheunen Street in Riga. The coachman Sachar and servant Otto were busy bringing the luggage from the second floor to the coaches. Under the seats, on the running boards and on the roofs, travel suitcases of all sizes were stored. Coats and blankets were put on the seats, and snacks and drinks went into the side pockets. Many hours had passed before everything was ready, and then four horses were hitched for each coach. Then the coachmen took their seats up front among many more small pieces of luggage.

This was not a trip to Ebelshof or the beach; it was a trip to a foreign country before the time of train service. It took one week to get from Riga to Berlin.

Ten people tried to find a comfortable place in the two coaches: father (Carl Boetticher), Mother (Emilie Boetticher), the grown-up daughters Linda and Amalie, the small Liselchen, the foster child Minna Lindenberg, the nanny Demoiselle Müller, the Bonne Ottieli Köhler, and last but not least the boys—Oskar (4) and Emil (3). Only the three older sons were left behind in Riga. They had to attend school. Miss Charlotte Buchholz looked after them, and Mr. Dr. Buchholz took over the duties of the father.

Mother's weakened health required a spa visit. Also, Amalie needed treatments for her foot. The spa in Kreuznach would be good for all travellers. Father only went along on this trip to be with his family. As soon as they had reached their destination, he would return to Riga because his business needed him. It took two visits to the healing water wells to have the full effect, so the plan was to come back in the summer of 1841, but in the meantime, they would visit Switzerland and during the wintertime stay in southern Germany. In the middle of 1841, Father would be back with his family to visit nice places, and they all wanted to be back home before the winter arrived.

It was not easy for Mother to leave Riga, but from early on, she had wanted to see the world with all the wonders created by God and by human hands. She left her well-organized household to other people. She would also miss her friends. But mostly she missed her three older sons: Carl, Friedrich, and Theodor for the next one and a half years. All her eight children were equally close to her heart. It was tough to say goodbye to the three boys, standing on the steps of the house, wanting to go along on this trip to see the unknown world! With tears in their eyes, they watched the coaches rolling away, turning right at the corner of Kalk Street, as their parents and siblings waved for the last time.

The travellers made their first stop in Mitau. Aunt Helene (Helene von Boetticher née von Reichard) took the opportunity to invite the guests on their way to Germany. Some friends from Riga had followed the travellers to join them for lunch and helped them to keep their spirits high at the festive table and ease the pain of separation.

After Mitau, the road led them through Courland's rich agricultural lands into the flat country of Lithuania. They spent the night in Schaulen where the girls especially took to the Polish way of life with humour. All in all, the atmosphere was great during this trip; the young girls with Miss Müller in the second coach had a lot of fun. The first coach with the parents, the boys, and the nanny kept a more quiet tone. Father made everyone sit up straight, and he was not impressed with the way things were done in the second coach. Miss Müller knew how to laugh and joke with the young, and if Mother wanted the company of one of her daughters, seats were exchanged, one boy for one girl. The boys had no problem with this arrangement, but the girls were not too happy with the strict order in the first coach.

The children were delighted as they arrived in Tilsit (on the Baltic Sea coast), leaving Lithuania behind. The contrast gave the girls a taste of what was to come in Berlin and Dresden. Nothing is written about the trip to Berlin ("Only the green surroundings of Elbing and Landsberg were good on the eye.")

The travellers got to Berlin on May 19, with ample time to watch the ceremony to put down the foundation of the Frederick the Great Memorial. Every day brought new and better things to see or enjoy during the six-day stay. During the visit to the museum and the drive to Charlottenburg and Kreutzberg and then through the Tiergarten, they "discovered" the large city.

Mother had visited Berlin 20 years ago and was surprised to see how much nicer the city had become, especially the country houses near Potsdam Gate and the Tiergarten. They also enjoyed the theatre a few times: "We saw," so writes Mother, "a nice ballet and heard Robert the devil, with the Löwe (Mrs.) as Isabella. The orchestra in the opera is beautiful. Both the male characters were not so well played as other times."

Before they left Berlin, the Sasse family invited the travellers. For many years, Father had maintained connections with them and now everyone was welcomed in their house in Pankow for a party in the evening in honour of the guests. Everyone enjoyed being among friends. Hotel life had not caught on yet.

They left Berlin behind on May 25 on the way to Leipzig. The coaches went from station to station, and one had more time to see nature compared to the travel with the train. To liven things up, the drivers would play a song on the "horn" to the delight of the boys.

The arrival in Leipzig was early, so it was decided to take the "steam wagon" to Dresden. The coaches and most of the luggage stayed behind. A short lunch and the whistle sounded for us to enter the train. We took our seats in this strange vehicle. Only after the train had moved slowly and surely out, did we start to relax. Quicker than we had ever travelled, we reached our destination later in the evening.

The beginning of the Woolmart and the holidays (Witsun) had brought many people to Dresden. All hotels were full in the city, and our parents were afraid we would have to spend the night on the street, but finally we got two rooms in the Hotel de Saxe.

The next morning, we awoke early to the sound of the church bells ringing, announcing the festive day. Quickly everyone was ready to go out, and the adults went to church where they listened to the sermon of Pastor Girardet. Shortly after, we all had lunch at the hotel, and in the afternoon, we went to the Linke Spa and Findlater Winery. Among all the many strange people, our little troupe felt a bit lost, but we really enjoyed the view across the River Elbe and the many nice villages beyond. The next day, we made the trip to Tharand. The road led through the Plauen area and was quite impressive. Now, for the first time, the younger generation saw mountains, which brought great delight. In Tharand, we visited with the von Tappe family. These friends of the family showed us a good time, and the day will always be remembered. The friendly Tappes went along to show their guests from Riga all the beautiful sights around Tharand. The day ended much too quickly, and it was time to say goodbye as we drove back to Dresden.

In Dresden, we had to visit different friends: the Falks, the Ulmers and especially the Kraukling family. Mother liked Mrs. Kraukling but also the children and Director Mr. Kraukling. His informal way of life impressed her. Under his guidance, we visited the historic museum, the picture gallery and the natural history collection. He was a great leader. The travellers spent happy evening hours with the Krauklings and their relatives.

The time in Dresden ended with a tour of the Saxon Switzerland (Sächsische Schweiz). Here are the words that Mother wrote about this trip:

On Thursday morning we left past Pillnitz into the Saxon Switzerland. In Lohman we arranged to have Amalie carried in a special chair. We visited the Lochmill and the Bastille on the way to Uttewald. We got there in time to enjoy the view and hoped for a good sunny morning. But it was somewhat foggy and only at times we were able to see the mountains and valleys. My thoughts went to all my loved ones I had left behind and quietly prayed to God. I had not slept the night before and felt stressed and so I rode with the children and let the others walk through the beautiful Amsel Valley. We drove from Rathewalde to the waterfalls behind Schandau. There, Malchen (Amalie) needed to be carried again, but the little boys went ahead happily. From the cow barn Boetticher (the Father) had rented a second seat that I took, or the children. We arrived on top of the large Winterberg. The weather was good and the view beautiful. The next morning at 6:00 we all left the Winterberg and drove through the rain to Herrnskretchen. Here a boat took us to Königstein where we had permission to walk into the fortress. We will forever remember the view from up there. The beautiful mountains that had been close or far during the last days were now spread out in a panoramic picture in the evening sun. It got late as we arrived in Dresden and everyone fell tired into bed.

It is easy to see from Mother's short report that everyone had a good time on this trip to Saxon Switzerland.

Nine days after Witsun, we took the steam wagon to Leipzig. It was a three-and-a-quarter-hour train ride. We stayed there two days and then left for Weimar. There lived the very good friend of the family Oberbürgermeister (Mayor) Carl Schwabe. This connection had lasted for 20 years through many letters and would continue right into old age with the good Schwabe and his friendly wife. After their death, Father still looked after his family.

The two coaches arrived late in the evening in Weimar. There the family took rooms in a hotel. Early the next morning, Mother got up with Liselchen and went to find the house of the Schwabes where she had spent many happy hours 20 years ago. But they had moved into a different place and she had to ask directions to find the way. "It was a happy reunion," Mother wrote, "the good Schwabes were just very nice people and we were invited to stay all day and they showed us Weimar with all the sights of the town. We stayed five days in Weimar."

The next goal was the Gutenberg printing press festivities in Mainz on the River Rhine, but on the way there, some time was needed to visit the Wartburg of Martin Luther near Eisenach. This castle was then not renovated with the wall paintings as we see it today. Nevertheless, it was interesting. The view from the hill higher up ("High Sun") was breathtaking. It had just rained, and the gray clouds opened up. A beautiful rainbow appeared in the sky, and on the winding way down, the Wartburg was surrounded by the rainbow. This unbelievable picture was very impressive.

One had hoped to be in Frankfurt in the next 24 hours. It had rained a lot and so the nights were cold and wet. Making the trip at night with the children sleeping was not a good idea. So in the evening in Hanau, we stayed for the night in the Riese. Being quicker than everybody else, Mother was outside the next morning to see the nice marketplace, the Esplanade, and the Resideze Castle. But more than monuments in the cities, the beauty of the vegetation there in the warmer climate of the south impressed Mother. Mother wrote on June 27, 1840,

> The road from Hanau to Frankfurt can truly be called a garden. The River Main makes the difference in climate. We saw barley and rye fields ready for the harvest. The best black cherries can be bought for 2–3 Kreuzer per pound and magnificent roses can be seen everywhere. How nice it is to live where the air is mild, if we could take along all things that the heart desires.

In Frankfurt, they stayed in the Hotel Paris. The festivities for the Gutenberg days were in full swing and a tent in front of the hotel showed different things about the printing business. The main action had taken place on the Ross Market. Here a statue of Gutenberg was unveiled with all the dignitaries of the city, the members of the guild, and the schoolchildren present. Everyone was singing the chorus, "Godfather, we praise you," under the thunder of cannons, and all the church bells were ringing.

They had to visit the cathedral, the Römer, the city museum, then onto Berthmann's Garden, they went. They took a drive on the promenade to the cemetery, which was so beautiful that Mother wrote it was "so nice that the living must think how great it would be to rest here forever." In the evening, the grown-ups went to the theatre to see *The Dungeons of Edinburgh*. The performance was good, but Mother missed two male characters and said, "Good thing we have very good actors and singers in Riga."

The parents got good advice about Kreuznach from friends of the family, the Pheils from Riga. At that time, the spa lacked some of the modern amenities. There the family would stay for a while (without Father), and the news about Kreuznach was not great. Getting there was no problem. Five times a day, the steam wagon left from Frankfurt to Mainz and took 50 minutes. From Mainz to Kreuznach (actually Bingen/Rhine), we could take the steamboat. So the coaches stayed in Frankfurt, and we got ready for the trip to Kreuznach.

Father came along with us to Kreuznach even though news from Riga told him that he was needed there. His oldest son, Carl, had a nervous sickness, and the parents were really worried. Even Mother wanted to come along, but she was in no shape to do so at that time. Father hurried home from Frankfurt—Weimar to Riga in seven days! He did not even take the time in Weimar to see the Schwabes. He passed through this city at night, the city he would have loved to stay in for a while. Back in Riga, he found his son in better shape than he had expected.

Chapter 2

Kreuznach and Schwalbach

Our travellers tried to get comfortable in Kreuznach and found an apartment in the city. It rained for the first eight days so no trip outside could be made. Then the sun came out, and they rented two horse coaches. Mother took the eight people on a trip to Rheingrafstein to see the beautiful view from the "goose." On foot, everyone went to the Saline Münster in the valley, and on the steep paths, the young boys walked very well. Across the Nahe River shore, they made a visit to the Ebern Castle with the few into the Nahe Valley, the Rothenfels, and the ruins of Kronberg. "We clearly saw how nice God's world is," wrote Mother at the end of her report, "and happy we all arrived back in Kreuznach at 8:00 in the evening."

In Kreuznach, everyone took the spa treatment and the baths and drank from the wells. This provided a good appetite for the children. In the beginning, contact with other people was missing. Here every guest went his or her way, but soon Mother made the acquaintance of the friendly Pastor Schneegans. The children were allowed to play in his garden, and the Pastor also introduced everyone to his brother, who was a guest at the spa. Among the many guests who filled all the hotels were also Prince Karl and his wife. His

Highness met the boys at one time, and Mother wrote to Father in Riga:

> The Prince and his wife went to a well one time and many people had followed them along on the promenade. Our little boys sitting on a bench were approached by the Prince's wife and asked about their names and who their Father is. Not shy at all, they gave their names and said about their Father: "He went to Riga to Mad. Andersohn and his name is Carl Boetticher." So tell the good Andersohn, the children think of her as we all do. She will be happy to hear that.

As we can see from the letters, the thoughts of Mother and the children went often to Riga. There, Father, if he was not occupied in the business, avoided the empty house and spent time with good friends. Every week, letters were sent between Riga and Kreuznach, but it took three weeks to get an answer to a letter. In July 1840, Mother wrote:

> I hope to get a letter from you, my dear husband. We can hardly wait! Tell our friends to also write to me. Don't forget to tell the Laubes, Kuehns, Thons and my Jette (Henriette Hartmann) that I think often of them. It was nice that the old Sachar welcomed you. This makes one feel at home ... Give

our boys a kiss on my behalf even though they often give me a hard time back home. I love them with all my heart. Thank Mad. Buchholz for all the care she gives you."

The spa life got pretty monotonous. The doctor had prescribed six more weeks, and this made the guests unhappy. They would have much preferred to go to Switzerland. But after this spa treatment, the next one was to be taken in Schwalbach. The weather was not great, but if possible, all went for hikes, most often to the Saline. Mother liked it there and made the decision during the spa visit next year to take rooms there instead of Kreuznach.

The children played often in Pastor Schneegan's garden but Mother was afraid they might eat the berries and grapes that grew there. Besides the many hikes, the older youth took part in dances. The daughters came home disappointed and never went again. Our Mother wrote: "Our dances at home are much nicer organized, and our girls are much better dancers than the kids here."

The spa treatments were done in July, and at the beginning of August, they left for the next spa in Langenschwalbach. Mother's patience was tested greatly by 11 weeks of spa life, and she really disliked being idle. On the way from Riga to Kreuznach, she was quite restless, and she had a hard time forgiving herself for having "produced only one sock on the drive to Berlin." She had problems with the fact that the children were not occupied on a regular basis. In her letters, she writes:

Lisinka is losing her knowledge of the ABCs but walks well, eats a lot of cherries and strawberries and plays well with the smaller children. When it comes to music, the young girls have a lot of catching up to do. We have one instrument but it is not used very often.

Even though the lazy lifestyle made her unhappy, she liked the healthy look of her children.

The children look great. Oscar is quite healthy, and Emil is often misbehaving. I feel strong, like I have not felt for years, and if my darling would see me now, he would be surprised. I often walked alone or I took Lisinka along. She is very quick on her feet.

Amalie still had problems with her foot; even in Schwalbach, she had pains. She only walked the way to the spa and then sat almost all day with the foot up to avoid the pain.

The weather turned nicer in Schwalbach, so they took more hikes. "The surroundings of this town are quite beautiful, and I like it here. The hills are forested with good walks and driveways."

Good news arrived from Riga about Carl's health. The doctors had prescribed a trip for the boy, and Father had decided to accompany his son, so one day both showed up in Schwalbach. They had travelled through Berlin and Weimar, and there they stayed two days at Schwabes. Carl looked good when he arrived in Schwalbach, and Mother was really happy to receive her loved ones.

By the end of September 1840, the Schwalbach spa treatment had ended. Longer trips were not planned for that year. Father had to go back to Riga, and Carl had to resume his studies. So in the fall of 1840, they made a tour past Ems to Koblenz, on to Düsseldorf, Eberfeld, and Remscheid. In Remscheid, they visited friends of the family, the von Berges. A son of this family had stayed in our parents' house in Riga on his way to Russia on business trips and was always a welcomed guest. From Remscheid, the trip went south to Koblenz and from there to Mainz on the steamship and on to Frankfurt by steam wagon. There the coaches took the family past Heidelberg and Mannheim to Karlsruhe.

The plan had been to stay over winter in Mannheim but to get a better education for the children, Karlsruhe was the place, especially to learn foreign languages. "As we reached Karlsruhe," Mother wrote, "we had plans to go to Lausanne for the winter because of the mild climate and for the kids to learn the French language. Mr.

Kruse, whose wife lived in Montreux, told us about the beautiful surroundings there and the children got all excited. But in the end, we stayed in Karlsruhe, so my husband could accompany us and help us move in. He had a long way back, especially this time of year."

Chapter 3

Karlsruhe

Mother found a completely furnished apartment in Karlsruhe. The owner, Mrs. von Weiler, had moved to Mannheim for the next half year. Mother wrote,

> We are happy to move from all the hotels into the von Weiler apartment and to feel at home. Tomorrow a new houseguest moves in, a young lady from Switzerland who speaks no German. Her name is Julie Grubert from Neuchatel and the French lessons will begin soon. As soon as Mr. von Weiler has moved out, the rooms will be used for music lessons for Lina. The girls have all intentions to work hard this winter, may God give them perseverance. It is easy to get outside. The weather is great (November 5, 1840), and the kids are outside playing. They like the way to the castle a lot. We hope the visits to the theatre will give us many nice evenings and have a good time here through the winter far away from Riga. I hope his friends invite my good husband often so that he does not have to spend the long winter evenings alone in his house. I picture giving my boys back home and all my

friends a big hug after an 11-month absence and my thoughts are always with them.

Mother found her daily routine in Karlsruhe, but her thoughts were with everyone back in Riga. A family, the Westbergs, had taken over the house in Ebelshof for the summer of 1840, and Pastor Taube and Councilman Eberhard Kuehn occupied the two smaller land houses.

A long and heartfelt letter arrived for Mother's birthday on September 7, 1840. All these and other friends had signed it, expressing their gratitude to know her and sending many best wishes along. When the letter arrived in Karlsruhe on October 28, 1840, it brought great joy. Father was still there but left ten days later with Carl for Riga. In Weimar, they saw the Schwabes, and in Dresden, they stayed a few days with the Baehr family, and then it was off to Riga.

Mother spent her time taking long walks, meeting friends, going to the theatre and dances and arranging the schooling of her children in music, language, and French literature. The young French lady, Julie Grubert, taught the boys in French, and in a few months, they had enough language skill to make small conversations. Mother wrote,

Karlsruhe, December 1840

Christmas Eve we first went to the Hausraths where I left some gifts for their children, and when we got home, our kids were surprised to see the tree all decorated with gifts under it. It is cold now—14 to 16 degrees and the small, stupid stoves need to be fed with coal constantly or the house gets cold quickly. The door of Mrs. von Weiler's place doesn't fit well, and one can see the daylight coming in. Two weeks ago, the Hausraths invited us for an evening. Eight girls were there, all former students of his. He is the most lovable teacher. Hausrath and his wife read us stories, and then we all sang together. At the Hausraths', we met a nice young girl, a Miss Fiess. She has a very good voice, and after Christmas, we invited her over and she and Lina sang together and are happy. If we get an invitation, we are glad and take it. New Year's Eve, Lina, Minna and I are going to a party.

Karlsruhe, January 30, 1841

Thank God we are all healthy. Oscar looks really well this winter. Emil lost some weight and is almost as tall as Oscar. If you were here, you would enjoy hearing them speak French, and Lisinka tries hard to use that language and was very busy in the last weeks. I correspond with many people everywhere and also with men. I know you want our children to take extra schooling, and now Malchen and Minna take classes in English with Miss Müller. When Professor Hausrath praised the English literature, Lina replied there is enough to read in German. You know that I greet all our friends back home, and therefore I don't have to name them to you.

Karlsruhe, February 6, 1841

You think I am too careful when it comes to spending money, but this is not true when I look at my bookkeeping. I just love to spend it on others rather than on myself. There are not too many ways to spend money here. It was quite cold in January, but on many occasions we went tobogganing. Now the weather is mild and the children are playing outside in the yard. Soon I will write to Dr. Prieger in Kreuznach to ask him to get us a three- to four-bedroom apartment near the Saline. I am teaching Oscar to read, and I am surprised how quickly he remembers the alphabet and the letters. He is a good boy and is happy to bring his book to read to me and wants to read to you soon. God keep our little boys. They are lovely children with the best genes. On sunny days, we are ready to fly away. In ten weeks, with God's will, we are back in Kreuznach.

Last night we went to the Hausraths'. We talked and sang, and we all listened to someone reading aloud. I like this custom and also that they only serve sandwiches, cold cuts and tea and sometimes a bit of cake. The young ones complained there was not enough food on the table.

Greet all our friends, stay healthy and go to bed before midnight. Again, warm regards.

Karlsruhe, February 18, 1841

Yesterday we spent a few very nice hours at the Hausraths'. There we met a Mr. Holzmann (who is a teacher for the youngest Prince), and he studies the Indian language. He had translated a poem from Sanskrit, which he now read for us. This language brings many pictures, and the verses sounded good. Sometimes Mr. Hausrath reads aloud or he sings with Lina or accompanies her on the piano. In short, the nice Hausrath spoils us and we miss his company after a very short time of absence.

From the many letters that Mother sent from Karlsruhe to Riga to be in contact with her husband and her sons, I picked these most important ones that show the life passed along during the winter months in Karlsruhe. Mother led, so to speak, a double life. On the one hand, her heart was with the family and friends in Riga, but she made new friends and enjoyed their interests. The letters that Father wrote back did not survive, but we read in Mother's letters on occasion that he did not have an easy time during her absence.

When Father got back to Riga, he had the builders in his house completely renovate the interior to make room for a large dance hall for the youth. In the meantime, Father occupied one small room for the night and during the day was in his office. He always loved to entertain his friends, but now they invited him over for the long winter evenings. Among the many letters written 50 years ago, we also find one from a daughter written to her father in December 1840.

December 16/28, 1840

Dearest Father! Your letter arrived here yesterday and brought great joy to young and old. It got here on the third Christmas day, and when we read it aloud, many tears were shed thinking of our good father and the brothers back home, not being with us for the first time in our lives. But still we had lots of fun, especially since the Holy Christ brought us a lot of gifts as always and we thank him with all our hearts.

Christmas Eve, we first went to the Hausraths' and received gifts there. Lisinka got a doll and the boys a hobbyhorse and a whip.

When we got home, our tree was up and that made us kids really happy because we did not expect any Christmas this year. Oscar and Emil screamed with happiness and also broke some of their toys right away. We older ones said our own funny poems, and the evening passed by with many jokes. Too bad, you, my dear Father, and the brothers were not here or any of our friends. We realized that it is only the 12th of December back home (difference in calendar), and you may not have thought about us at all.

Life in Karlsruhe is not really as bad as we had thought at first. During the week, we are busy with music, we read in French or go for walks. On Sundays the Hausraths or the Welziens come for a visit, and everyone is in a good mood. Mr. Hausrath introduced me to a young lady, Miss Fiess, a talented person with a good upbringing and an excellent voice. But Mr. Hausrath is just the best. He comes over daily, brings a book along, or sings with us. We learned a lot of French from Julie, the French girl, and Emil especially thinks it sounds better to speak that language and often corrects Oscar. If you meet them now, they will probably talk French to you. Both boys just walked up to my desk and said to tell you to thank the Holy Christ. Oscar also tells you he was not always a good boy, but Emil claims the opposite.

We often thought what you could give the boys (at home) for Christmas and came to the conclusion that a poetry collection, written by G. Schwab, would be a gift for Friedrich, and we are sure that Carl and Theodor would like some good books also. Mr. Buchholz, I'm sure is happy to help.

Goodbye, my loving Father, greetings from all your children, Miss Müller and Julie, with love from your daughter …

To the brothers a thousand greetings and kisses.

When reading these letters time and again, we read the name Pastor Hausrath. He was a court preacher and a well-known chancellor. He was also a man with a brilliant mind and broad education. He was a great conversationalist as well. Everyone who knew him liked him a lot, and his gift in music, song and piano, was outstanding. This gifted man had great influence on the Boetticher family, the old and the young. The girls were mad about him, and Mother admired him. A busy man, he always found time for our family in Karlsruhe.

Towards the end of the winter months, Mother wrote:

I am happy with the time we spent here with all the good friends, even so, had we stayed in Dresden in the company of the Kybers and the Baehrs and their Riga atmosphere, I don't think we would have had a better time. The winter is over soon and we will fly away like birds in the spring.

Daughter Lina and foster daughter Minna visited the theatre, concerts and dances. Malchen had to stay home with her bad foot, but Mother looked to entertain her. Lisinka had home schooling from

Miss Müller, and Mother taught her two young sons, Oscar and Emil, how to read and write.

Mother not only dealt with her family in Karlsruhe during the week but wrote many letters to all kinds of friends. Most, of course, went to her loving husband with little notes to her dear friend Jette Hartmann, some of which are still around. Here she opened up all her inner thoughts to her girlfriend in Riga.

Before leaving Karlsruhe for good, the family had plans to make a trip to the Black Forest.

The teaching job with Julie Grubert was terminated, and instead a French lady from Genf, Switzerland, was hired. A few months later, this very educated, sophisticated lady, Madame Ernestine Maraz, started to work for the Boetticher family, and everyone liked her.

In the middle of April, a young friend of the family, Hermann Pacht, came to visit. His plan was to travel to France, but he changed his mind. He now went along with everyone on a tour through Baden (southwest Germany) and then to walk to Stuttgart and onto Halle to study theology.

About this trip through Baden, Mother wrote:

We left Karlsruhe on April 26, 1841, to see Baden and its surroundings. The weather was beautiful. I have heard many nice things about this area and all expectations that I had were met. We saw the Merkur, the old castle Baden, Ebersteinburg, Ebersteinschloss, the Yburg and the beautiful river Murgvally to Forbach. The view from the higher mountaintops was so spectacular that it was tough to move on. We were back in Karlsruhe on May 2 with new energy in all the fresh air.

After packing the luggage and saying their goodbyes, the family left the place where they had lived for six months on May 7. "I am thankful to leave this city behind. God kept us all healthy, and even Malchen's foot healed well and is now pain-free."

On the way to Kreuznach, the travellers went first to Heidelberg for two and a half days. Under blue skies, they made a trip to Königstuhl and Neckarsteinach and to the old beautiful castle. Two of Pastor Hausrath younger brothers, students at Heidelberg University, were our companions, and also Hermann Pacht showed up. He had walked from Stuttgart to Heidelberg to be with the travellers for a few days. "The castle ruin was nice and how beautiful the valley to Neckargemünd and the way to Neckarsteinach were. The air was rich with the smell of flowers and one saw the hills far away in the clear air," Mother wrote about this trip to Heidelberg. One must remember what made this trip so enjoyable was the presence of the three young jolly students.

Chapter 4

Second Kreuznach Spa Treatment and Schwalbach

Mother arrived with her crew in Kreuznach on the evening of May 10, 1841. Dr. Prieger had gotten them an apartment by the Saline. Now they lived in the country, not like the year before in the city. It was a good spot; up front was a garden, and behind the house was a hill with a forest. During the hot time of the day, one could cool off at the Saline close by. Everybody liked it there, especially the thought that Father would join them soon. Mother wrote the following:

> Now we live totally out in the country, the drinking fountain is in the garden and Kreuznach is a half hour from here. We often drink a glass (of spa water) here, the next one in the Karlshall and the third on the Bath Island outside the city, then we walk slowly home to get a very good appetite for breakfast. Our landlady, Mrs. H. has three lovely daughters and with other girls in the neighborhood, my girls have lots of new friends.

The month of May brought beautiful weather, and Mother and the children felt happy there. Her thoughts were often with her husband, and in her letters, she told him not to delay his visit to Kreuznach. Letters from home brought good news.

To everyone's surprise, old Mr. Schwabe from Weimar showed up in Kreuznach. He was with his brother, the Russian Czar's physician S. and his wife at the spa in Wiesbaden, and the desire to see the Boettichers had brought him there. He was greeted with such enthusiasm that the landlady thought Father had arrived from Riga. Plans were made for a trip; Schwabe and the Boettichers would go to Switzerland and the northern part of Italy. During this time, Oscar and Emil were to stay with Miss Ottilie in the house of Mrs. Schwabe in Weimar. Everyone was enthusiastic about this tour to the south and hoped for a good outcome.

At the end of May, Mother moved to Schwalbach (spa) to continue drinking the water there. During the Witsun holidays, she made an excursion with her children to the pretty Niederwald (forest) and then to Rüdesheim/Rhine. There she left the family to go back to Kreuznach with Miss Müller and travelled on to Biebrich and Wiesbaden, as Mr. Schwabe had invited her. Back in Schwalbach, she took a room in the Hotel Stadt Mainz with a view of the wine fountain and the bathhouse, which would remind her to take the spa water and baths with great punctuality. Mother was always healthy, but in the last years before she left Riga, she had had some aches and pains. She was determined to get home in the best shape possible.

She wrote, "I will drink lots of iron and steel and bathe in it so I get as strong as this metal when I am back in Riga."

The beautiful spring weather had left. The strong winds and cold made everybody wear coats to take the walks required by the treatment. Even the boys had to play inside. Many letters were written between Kreuznach and Schwalbach.

In June 1841, Mother got a letter from Riga that said that Father would be in Schwalbach in about 18 days. She was overjoyed and wrote, "I expect you here soon and then we'll travel together to the Saline to greet the children. May God be with you on your voyage, truly, your wife, Emilie."

Even though the weather was not great, Mother and Minna L. went to see Bad (spa) Ems on the River Lahn, to see this city where she had been 20 years earlier as a young woman for spa treatments. She wrote,

> I was happy to see the improvements that had been made. The near riverbed of the Lahn had been widened to make room for new buildings. The new spa house and colonnade are truly beautiful. Still, I am happy not to take the treatment here, because of the cramped conditions. A few more excursions into the surroundings ended the day and I was happy to be back in Schwalbach.

According to Father's letters, the spa treatments had worked well on Mother. She was able to walk longer distances without getting tired, her face had a nice colour, and her overall health had greatly improved. So she felt ready for the long trip to the Alps and Italy just like her daughters.

Father was due to arrive in Schwalbach at the beginning of July, and Mother could hardly wait. Every time a coach went by, she ran to the window. It was already getting dark on this day, the fifth of July; the town was quiet, when she heard far away the post horn signal. She rushed to the window. The coach had stopped in front of the hotel Stadt Mainz, and three people got out. She recognized Father's voice, and soon she was in her husband's arms. He had brought along a young lady from Riga, Miss Sophie Hielbig, with the travel destiny of Amsterdam, and in Wiesbaden, he had picked up Mr. Schwabe.

One can only imagine this joyful reunion. There was a lot to talk about, and then there were the questions about the boys back home, the friends, the house, and the servants. It was late before everyone got to bed for a rest after the long voyage. The new arrivals stayed an extra day and then drove through Schlangenbach to Kreuznach for a very happy reception.

The next days were used to get ready for the departure from Kreuznach. But before that, Father, as the travel guardian of Sophie

Hielbig, took her to Amsterdam. Daughter Lina and old Schwabe, always ready for a trip and to see this city of commerce came along, too.

During their nine-day absence, Mother and her crew went to Bingen/Rhine. There, on July 16, 1841, people celebrated the 25th year of unification of the Rhineland after freeing this country from the occupation of the French. The celebrations were in full swing. Every steamship going by, decorated with many flags, was greeted with six shots from the cannon on shore, and the ships returned this salute.

From Bingen, they made a few excursions. Mother wrote to Jette H. on July 1841:

> Yesterday we spent a few hours watching the beautiful illumination on the Rochusmountain. The River Rhine was lit up and the many islands looked very pretty in the distance right up to Biebrich. The many steam- and sailboats and the lush shores made this mighty river look even more enchanting. On the other side we saw the rich Nahevally (River) and far away the Donnerberg, which dominates all other hills. Twice I went to the Niederwald to look at the (ruin) Rossel with the temple. Two days ago we drove to Lorch and then into the Sauervally and after one hour arrived at the nice castle

Sickingen. In the afternoon we took the steamboat back to Bingen.

After Father was back from Amsterdam, the family left Bingen for Mainz. They took the left shore along the Rhine, and the view from Nieder-Ingelheim along the rich Reingau was spectacular. Mother was sorry to leave this beautiful place. In Mainz, after the six-hour drive, everyone rested and made plans for the trip to the south. Father took the boys to Frankfurt, where they left the coaches, and from there, the sons left with their Nanny Ottilie in the smaller travel wagon for Weimar. The parents trusted Ottilie with the care of their boys and knew Mrs. Schwabe in Weimar would look after them very well. Father brought back the larger coach, and including Mr. Schwabe, eight people had to fit in. He would have liked to buy a larger vehicle but could not find one in time. To make room, they had to leave a lot of luggage behind. Five grown-ups and little Lisinka fit inside and two people had to sit up front next to the driver.

The trip led from Mainz to Strassburg and Schaffhausen to Zürich and Luzern, then to Lausanne, Genf, and into the Chamonix Valley across the Simplon-Pass to the Lago Maggiore. They went further to see Mailand, Verona, and wonderful Venice. On the way back, they took the Etschroad across the Brenner-Pass to Tyrol and Salzburg.

They stayed in München for a visit and then went on to Linz and Vienna. There they rested and went sightseeing in the old Kaiser City. Past Prague, they reached Dresden, and now it was time for the trip back to Riga.

Unfortunately, I, the author (Emil), have not been able to write about this trip through the Alps and Northern Italy. I am sure that Mother, during the three-and-a-half-month tour, wrote many letters. But none have been found from that time, and no other reports have been located either.

Oscar and Emil had very few memories about their time in Weimar. They were just too young. But they enjoyed the freedom and had a really good time. They always remembered the friendly, loving guardian mother, Mrs. Schwabe.

It was late in the fall of 1841. The floating bridge into Riga to connect the shores of the River Düna (Daugava) was still in use. One day, two coaches with four horses each crossed this bridge towards the city through the narrow castle gate to the Scheunen Street and the Boetticher house. Now 11 people got out because the family had brought along Miss Ernestine Maraz, a French lady from Switzerland.

During the one-and-a-half-year absence, the house had been totally remodeled. The friends and relatives all met there again for a good time.

From the boxes and suitcases, many precious items to beautify the living space were removed, but all were small treasures compared to the precious memories everyone brought back from this trip. "Lasting," Mother said about such ownership. Even though nobody who had bought these treasures is alive, the memories from the years 1840 and 1841 had to be written 50 years later.

Part III

From the Silver Anniversary to the End

Chapter 1

Getting Comfortable in the House

Family Life

It was a happy reunion after one and a half years of absence, but soon it was time to decorate all the rooms in the now remodeled house on Scheunen Street in Riga. The second floor had 12 rooms and the third three large ones, and there, Father and the older sons moved in. The second floor rooms were more spacious now for all the female members and the two young boys. There also were the salons, the dance hall with four windows, the comfortable Red Room and the small Blue Room, and all were well remembered by the people who saw them.

The large household consisted of the parents, the adult daughters Caroline (Lina) and Amalie (Malchen); the adopted daughter, Wilhelmine (Minna) Lindenberg; the ten-year-old daughter, Elise (Lisinka); the adult son Carl; and the younger sons Friedrich, Theodor, Oscar and Emil. The German governess, Miss Caroline Müller, a lovely, well-educated lady, taught the younger children and was intellectually involved with the older ones. The French governess brought along from Switzerland, Miss Ernestine Maraz, was now part of the family. She was young, beautiful and educated, and she took part in all the family functions. A nanny looked after the small boys Oscar and Emil. Including the lower personnel were the driver, the servants, the female chef and for emergencies the widow Katharina Hintersdoff. It was a small army that Mother led.

Even though the house had a luxurious interior and many servants, life at the Boettichers was simple and plain. Father liked some glamour in his surroundings but for Mother this was not important to her and she looked for "peace that comes from the heart, that outer things cannot take away."

So she watched that her children were brought up without many possessions but knew the value of intellectual interests. This direction and idea gave the house a special atmosphere. Besides Mother, Miss Müller also looked to enrich the intellectual life in the Boetticher house, something unusual at that time in the Riga merchant circles. Life was not always joyful even though there were a lot of fun times. The underlying tone was a deeper, more serious one. The children were brought up with a deep sense of duty, and here the parents set a great example. Strict was the choice of friends of the children and the way they spent their spare time.

At the time the daughters entered adulthood, the theatre in Riga had great success under the leadership of Mr. Holtei. The members of the family enjoyed many performances of the actors and singers. It was customary among the rich merchant houses to invite the actors over for parties, but the parents did not allow their daughters to attend any of those. Gossip about the theatre performers was not allowed at home, and Mother strictly enforced this "no gossip" rule. Every guest of the family noticed this intellectual custom and made comments about it. "It is so nice here without the usual gossip!" This is from a friend of one of the daughters who took part in the conversations at the Boettichers' years ago.

Chapter 2

Daughters and Sons, Marriage of the Two Older Daughters, The Sons-in-Law: Kuehn and Pacht

At the social gatherings, after getting back from the trip, the centre of attention was the older daughters. Lina, musically gifted with a strong mind, was like a younger friend to Mother. She was a lovely person with a deeply religious mind.

The second daughter, Amalie, was a bit younger but had a different character. She had spent part of her youth with the family Pacht in Wolmar. Her hearing problems brought limitations in her education. So her life had turned more to the inside. With a rich imagination, keen sense of observation, and a soft heart, she was always thankful to receive the good things of life. She was happy to help others and kind; she never complained and had a good sense of humor.

Combining the characters of the two girls would show us a picture of Mother.

The foster child, Wilhelmine Lindenberg, was adopted in 1835 and since then treated as one of the children. Minna had a very soft, thankful nature, with a great sense of duty—this came quite natural to her. Always happy and friendly, she showed great interest in the people around her.

In the circle of grown-ups in the year 1842 belonged Carl, the oldest son. He went to the gymnasium (high school) at that time. Not quite healthy (he showed signs of depression), he gave the parents some worries. A person guided by his feelings, not a man of action, he liked the easy lifestyle. With a soft nature, he was musically gifted with a very good tenor voice, and he often sang for his audience.

The four younger sons and the third daughter were back at school; actually the two youngest were not even in school yet. Mother took great care of them, leading and guiding them through these early years of their lives. Just like the older siblings, these younger ones were all different in character. Even as a boy, Friedrich had daring thoughts, which took him far out past the world of reality. Theodor, on the other hand, liked the practical part of life and did not care about theories or philosophies. He enjoyed all the things he saw or could grip with his hands and roamed with his father's horses from the stable. Friedrich and Theodor took totally different roads through life, but they both loved the friendship and adoration of their youngest sister, little Lisinka, who was always friendly and loving to everyone. In age, she was closer to the two youngest brothers, and they would play together. For Oscar and Emil, too, Lisinka was the most liked sister. With her, they talked about the problems they encountered in their early lives.

After returning to Riga, the family's connections to old and new friends were renewed. To name all those who received the friendly hospitality of the Boettichers would take too long. For a long time, the family had close connections to the families of Kuehn in Eckau and Pacht in Wolmar. Mother had spent part of her youth in the Pastor's house in Eckau with the Kuehns. They were preachers there for many generations, and the brother of the Pastor was a friend of our father. Amalie, as a child, had lived for a number of years with the Pacht family in Wolmar. There Doctor Pirs Walter had lived; he looked after Amalie's foot problem. From those times, a great friendship developed between Mother and Mrs. Pacht, who was a sister of Dr. Prof. Pirs Walter.

Many letters were written to and from Eckau and Wolmar, and the families visited often. This interest was also shared with the next generation—a son of the Pastor in Eckau married the oldest daughter, Amalie, and a son of the Pachts' married the second daughter.

These events happened years apart, but there is some similarity because it was the friendship of the fathers in one case and the friendship of the mothers in the other that led to the marriages of their children.

Ernst Kuehn was born on June 18, 1814, in Eckau and studied theology from 1833 to 1836 in Dorpat (Tartu) and then in Halle (Germany). He was first a house teacher for the von der Ropp family in Pokroi (Province Kowno) for two years and from 1841 a preacher in Kruthen near Libau. Father liked his noble character and his teaching capability and asked him in 1841 for advice as an educator about the upbringing of his oldest son Carl. At this time, he learned a lot about the teaching method and mind of the young pastor.

In January 1842, Ernst Kuehn travelled to Riga, and shortly thereafter, Lina and he were engaged. This engagement did not last very long because the wedding took place on April 30, 1842, in the newly renovated rooms in the house on Scheunen Street with music and dancing. A few days later, the 20-year-old wife of the Pastor moved to Kruthen at the time of a beautiful spring. The blessings of the parents went along with their beloved daughter, who now lived far away at the side of her husband.

We now jump ahead five years to write about the engagement and marriage of the second daughter, Amalie.

Hermann Pacht, born April 25, 1816, in Wolmar, studied theology in Dorpat (Tartu) from 1835 to 1840 and then in Halle (Germany) from 1841 to 1842. Thereafter he was a teacher with the von Stryck family in Pollenhof for a few years. In 1846, he was appointed Pastor for Kokenhusen and Kroppenhof, and this position he held for 33 years. At the time when Amalie lived at the Pacht house, the oldest son Hermann was a high school student in Dorpat but spent his holidays at home. There he met Amalie, who was treated like a daughter of the family, and the young people became friends. This friendship was renewed when they met again in Karlsruhe and Heidelberg. He went along on the trips with the Boettichers through the Black Forest and the Neckar Valley.

An illness made Hermann move back to his parents' from Halle during the winter of 1841–42, and it took a while before he was back at work as a house teacher. Amalie and he did not meet again for a long time, but when he was appointed as pastor in Kokenhusen, he wrote a letter to Amalie confessing his love for her.

During the time of Amalie's engagement, Hermann's mother died. The wedding was celebrated quietly at Ebelshof on September 6, 1847. The uncle of the couple Bishop Dr. Ferd. Walter conducted the ceremony, and a few days after, the newlyweds moved to the pretty Kokenhusen.

Chapter 3

Separation from the Children, Old and New Relationships, Life in Ebelshof and Riga

In the five years between the marriages of the two oldest daughters, many changes had taken place in the house of the parents. Up to this time, they had all their children around and they were their main interest. Lina had left her parents' house first, but soon others followed her. In the summer of 1842, the third son, Theodor, left to live with Pastor Brasch in Niederbartau to continue his education. In January 1843, the oldest son, Carl, left to go to university. In January 1846, the second son Friedrich followed, and in August 1847, the two youngest sons, Oscar and Emil, left to get their education from Pastor Albanus in Dünamünde and later Engelhardshof. The same year, Amalie left her parents' house, which by this time had become very quiet. But then Theodor moved back home to go to school at the gymnasium (high school) in Riga. The last couple of years, he was educated by Pastor Boetticher in Bauske. After Amalie got married, Theodor and Lisinka and also the foster child Minna Lindenberg lived with their parents to keep them company.

At the same time as Lina with her young husband had moved to faraway Kruthen (May 1842), the family in Riga prepared to live in Ebelshof. This kept Mother very busy, but still her thoughts were always with Lina, and the separation from her was painful. The large exchange of letters with her oldest daughter showed this clearly.

Mother loved and enjoyed the many people around her and things that brightened up her life. "It is beautiful here," she wrote on May 21, 1842, from Ebelshof.

> The chestnut and apple trees are in full blossom and the air is rich with the smell of spring. I see the pretty green of the trees and hear the birds singing. Aunt Juli (Mrs. Kuehn) usually comes over in the morning for a few hours when Miss Müller is teaching. Sunday noon Madame Andersohn and Natalie (Wichmann) were here and in the afternoon the Pfeils came to visit for a few hours to enjoy our pretty garden. Natalie (Kleberg) comes on Wednesday to give Elise lessons. Yesterday Hensel was here with her three children. They had a lot of fun, and the children are nice. And on Sunday the Hartmanns were here too for a few hours. Too bad Jette (Miss J. Hartmann) has such little time this year.

Mother embraced all her many friends and relatives and opened her heart, but her birthday was a special day for all. The seventh of September saw a big celebration, and many remembered this day.

The following is a letter written by Mother on September 10, 1842, to Lina Kuehn about this occasion.

Many people came to visit on my birthday. The Hartmanns came over on Sunday already. Early in the morning, the band played music, and as I stepped outside, all the members of the family and my friends were waiting. In front of the house, everything was decorated with flowers and greens. I felt overwhelmed. The band played all day, and many more friends arrived. I thought of you and really would have liked to have you here. The weather was beautiful and the day passed quickly. After darkness there were fireworks in front of the house, and Carl and Friedrich especially liked the light balls. Then the group followed the band through the park (they played in different spots), because the night was so nice and mild ... How is Theodor? I missed my good boy on the 7th.

The children's birthdays too were celebrated very festively at Ebelshof. The large garden, festively decorated, held a great attraction for them.

When the fall winds blew the yellow leaves off the trees, the nightly frost changed the colours of the flowers, and the evenings got too cold to be outside at Ebelshof, it was time to move back to the city. Usually the other families (Mayor Kuehn and Pastor Taube, later also Superior Pastor Poeschau) who all lived on Ebelshof, had moved back already before the parents. Mother just loved to live in the country, and Father, after his daily work in the city, enjoyed his country estate very much.

If there were some friends around, they would play billiards in an old-fashioned room in one of the garden houses, and the little boys felt important by helping set up the balls. After supper, Father walked through the park, and if the moon was not out, the lanterns in the trees and bushes showed him the way.

But city life also had its pleasures, starting at the end of September. At the time when at Ebelshof the family would meet on the large porch to enjoy the cool air of the evening and to smell the fragrance of the beautiful oleander, in the city, the lamp "on the table in front of the red sofa" was lit and all sat together to listen to "Müllerchen" or Minna reading aloud from a good book. The young boys played nearby, and time passed quickly when somebody remembered that there were tickets for the theatre. The Boetticher family circle enjoyed the theatre visits very much but was quite selective about seeing the best performances. They had season tickets, but if nobody wanted to go or leave "the table with the red sofa," the tickets were taken to the Holy Ghost, and Natalie Wichmann was happy to receive them.

As someone read aloud, the hands were not idle. It would be interesting to know how many socks Mother knitted every year. Here the daughters could not compete. They did embroidery because it made for great gifts at birthdays, Christmas, and weddings. Father got many of the artworks from his daughters but had very little need for them, so they all ended up in a glass closet neatly arranged. The younger children often viewed this rich "art museum" with great interest. At the silver wedding anniversary of Uncle and Aunt Thonn in 1842, Malchen and Minna had sewn a large chair for them, and this was for a long time after a very important part of her furniture; a person who had to be honoured for any reason had to sit in this chair. This happened to a certain nephew who was not allowed to smoke at home (or Mother would say, "Cat eats hay"). At a visit, he had to sit in this honour chair, a drink in one hand and a cigarette in the other, and was told, "I like to see you smoke, you look so manly."

In the Christmas season, all the family members were busy making gifts. This included the younger ones. "The little boys," Mother wrote November 1844, "have besides the school hours only Christmas on their minds. This time they want to make many things. I had to give them money a few times for rubber and paper and such because there is a lot of glue, cardboarding and cutting going on. But they are still good-hearted boys and easy to manage."

The three youngest children did not take part in the conversations at the time of the sofa table. Nevertheless, Mother paid close attention to them. In almost all her letters to her oldest daughter, she writes about them. She wrote about Lisinka's enthusiasm for playing the piano or Oscar's good behaviour or when the two little boys sang their songs so nicely. She wrote about a situation on March 25, 1843, "Now Oscar sits across from me and is busy stitching on canvas, concentrating hard, never looking up. Lisinka does not want to play with the big doll anymore and says it is no fun to carry around something that has no life."

Chapter 4

Education of the Sons, Choosing the Occupations

Mother followed the education of her children with keen interest. Instruction in religion was a big part of it.

The sons had a free hand to choose their education, but only after finishing high school. The parents knew whoever had studied hard and "put all his soul" into his chosen job would find success. But these "jobs" were not to be felt as straitjackets. The occupations had to fit their individual dispositions and talents. Anyone who had made the wrong choice should make changes in time and not spend his life toiling in the wrong profession. This was a liberal approach by the parents because they knew that young people rarely knew where their talents lay before getting deeper into the world of employment. While in school, it is rare for a young person to know which road to take when it comes to a future occupation.

Certainly the parents would have liked to see their oldest sons stay in their chosen occupations after university. But true to their thinking, the sons were free to choose different roads. All of them, except for the youngest, switched to become agriculturalists, some forever, and some later turned to different adventures. Nevertheless, the parents helped them to establish themselves in the farming business.

In the beginning of the year 1848, Carl, without finishing his studies at the university in Dorpat, left for Germany to learn the practical part of farming. Father, in the meantime, bought the estates Pommusch and Arzen in Courland, which Carl took over after he came back in 1849. Towards the end of 1848, Friedrich too left the University in Dorpat. His conviction pulled him a lot to the newly awakening German fatherland; his thoughts and feelings pulled him away from the small surroundings of his birthland. He left in March 1849 to move to an agriculture school in Broesa near Bautzen, which was established and run by his future brother-in-law, later a professor in Jena (Germany) but then living in Bautzen, Dr. Ernst Stoeckhardt. The year after, with Father's financial help, he bought the knights manor Zschillichau near Bautzen. He managed this estate for four years with great enthusiasm and then sold it to follow his intellectual nature and settled in Dresden.

Theodor, after finishing high school, decided to become a merchant. His apprentice years started in Riga with the merchant house Wilhelm Strauss & Co. He left in March 1850, stayed in Germany for a short time and then moved to England where he lived in Hull and London to further his education as a merchant. But then he too found his love for farming and left England for an estate near Magdeburg (Germany) to learn the new trade. After he moved back to Latvia in 1853, he continued his education in Mesothen. A year later, the estates Arzen and Pommusch were separated and Carl became the owner of Pommusch and Arzen became Theodor's estate.

This is the way the parents helped their sons to establish their own households. At the same time, the education of the younger ones had to be completed. The older sons went to school in Riga, Theodor was educated in the country before he moved back to Riga to go to high school. Now the two youngest boys were not to stay in Riga for further schooling, but the parents wanted a good teacher for private schooling at home. They asked their son-in-law Ernst Kuehn to find a candidate. The new pedagogue was quite young, but the parents thought this could be an advantage, as his age would help create a good friendship with the sons. He started teaching in the summer of 1845, but the choice of this candidate was a bad one. His teaching method was terrible and often rough and lazy. He gave his pupils work to do in the classroom and then used his spare time to play the flute next door, telling them to keep quiet about this or they would be punished. The parents had no clue about all of this, and Mr. S. acted as if they had given their approval for him to teach this way. That was why the boys never told their parents about their mistreatment.

But then the story leaked out and the house teacher left quickly. The boys were happy to see him go.

Both moved to Pastor Albanus in Dünamünde where they received a good education with love and friendship by excellent teachers.

Chapter 5

Old Friends

The mind's eye sees all the people who could be found often at the Boetticher house. The circle of friends and acquaintances was large. "It is nice," Mother said, "to know that other hearts are happy when we are, or sad when we are grieving." These people were closest to her, and the parents welcomed them at any time without invitation.

Here we have to mention the old "Madame Anderson" (born March 18, 1762; died June 1843). In her younger years, she had seen better days. Now as a widow, she lived in the Convent to the Holy Ghost and had to be happy with those accommodations. Her income was minimal, and what she needed now she had to create with her busy hands. Always happy and optimistic, she was well liked at the Boettichers' as a guest for Christmas and all other festivities. Never separated from her lantern and her cane in her hand, the old Anderson, with Natalie at her side, walked over from the Holy Ghost to the main house if she wanted conversation. Her Natalie was loved by all the Boetticher children and treated as one of them. When the old lady died at 81, everyone was sad.

The next friend of the house was the elderly Miss Friedericke Kuehn, a sister of the Eckau Probst K. and the mayor of Riga K; she was also an aunt of the pastor in Kruthen. She lived in two rooms in the Boetticher house, facing the backyard, and from her window, she could wave greetings to the Boettichers. Intellectually very bright and quick-witted but friendly, she gave the children music lessons. Success in this field would have been greater, but her soft nature let the kids get away with many pranks. She loved tall, good-looking men and was fascinated by General-Gouverneur Survornow. The old miss was treated like family, and old and young called her "Friederike." She was like an aunt with all her oddness and missed very much when she moved to live with her brother, the Mayor Kuehn, after he became a widower. So the friendly greetings from her window were gone and the visits with the Boettichers almost stopped. Soon after Mother had died, her old friend Friedericke Kuehn left this life also; as she got ready to go to Mother's funeral, she suddenly passed away.

Whoever attended the happy dance evenings in the house of the Boettichers 40 to 50 years ago will remember the so-called Red Room next to the ballroom. There some elderly ladies sat watching the youth, talking about the times of now and of the past. Most of them could look back half a century; they too used to be excellent dancers, and now they used more or less ruthless criticism on the efforts of others. Mrs. Anna Caroline Thonn was one of them.

The Boetticher children respected her as if she were one of their parents, because she was Mother's stepsister and as such had to be treated with respect. One time, Oscar got into deep trouble when he greeted her jokingly, "Good day, my lovely Caroline," the way Mother would do.

Aunt Thonn and her husband were always invited to the festivities. She was born March 15, 1787, and was 30 years old when she got married. Her hair turned white soon after, and according to the fashion of that time, she wore a wig. Mother was 12 years younger, but they had a good relationship even though the aunt gave her free advice often, especially to dress better and spend more on toiletries, but Mother did as she liked. She used to love to dance in her youth and could not understand why the polka was not invented then. Her apartment was very clean and well organized, and their uncle's love of flowers was visible everywhere. She was a generous person. Her guests received the best the house had to offer—silver cutlery and the best crystal. Uncle Thonn not only loved flowers but was an admirer with great knowledge of music. A male quartet with the names Niemann, Bornhapt, Rudolff and Kranich practiced and sang often in his house. These gentlemen belonged also to the Boettichers' circle and created many happy hours of entertainment there.

The closest friend of our mother was her girlfriend Henriette Hartmann, called "Aunt Jette" by the children. She was the perfect example of an old maid. We will talk about her friendship with Mother at another time.

Among the men who were seen at the Boettichers' besides Uncle Thonn was a relative of Father's, his brother-in-law Lösevitz, who was married for the second time to Auguste Pohrt.

Highly revered and loved by the Boettichers was the old mayor Eberhard Kuehn (born April 23, 1775; died July 11, 1858). A modest man and hard worker with great knowledge, he knew how to listen rather than talk. In the year 1800, he started his work for the City of Riga after studying law. In 1850, the citizens celebrated his 50 years of service in a great fashion with him. He loved the peace and quiet of the country at Ebelshof, where he lived during the warmer months in the Kuehns' house. Not only at Ebelshof but also in Riga, Father loved his company. After his wife died, his sister Friedericke moved in with him and looked after his household.

Totally different than the mayor was his brother, the Probst in Eckau, Ernst Kuehn. A tall, large man, he impressed with his appearance. He was a man that only "God's Land" Courland could produce. His loving wife, Julie (née Thonn), was 96 years old when she died, mentally sharp right to the end—a ray of sun for everyone around her. The Kuehns came to visit the Boettichers every time they were in Riga, and this was now more often, after Lina got married.

There are more relatives in the wider circle that we have to mention. One son of Aunt Kyber's, Ferdinand, lived in Riga. From 1815–1817, he studied in Dorpat and managed the paper factory Ligat in Riga. Another son, Albert, was also a manager there, and a third, Eduard, was owner of the estate Paltemal. The last two were married to two sisters, Olga and Elise von Wrangell. Ferdinand was not married and was a member of the Compagnie of Schwarzenhäupter in Riga. He was often seen in the Boetticher house. Later in life, he gave up his bachelor position.

Chapter 6

Relatives of Father, Uncle Johan, Aunt Minna

Father's relatives lived mostly in Courland. His much younger brother Johann, owner of the estate Kukschen, seldom travelled but exchanged many letters with Father, who looked after the business for him in Riga. Uncle Johann trusted Father's good business sense and effort. He was a highly talented and scholarly man, but his hypochondriac inclinations made him avoid other people. The more he lost the positive outlook on life, the rougher his letters to his brother became. Here is a nicer one on Father's birthday.

> I hope and wish that you, with the beginning of this spring, will be in good health and that you are in as good a shape with 80 as you are now with 70 years. God will look after all the rest! All the best to your loving wife and your family from me and my wife, your true brother.

Father and his brother Johann did not see each other often, but his two sons Carl and Friedrich, when they went to school in Riga, were always Sunday guests at the Boettichers'. Between them and their cousins in Riga, there was a lasting friendship. The Kukschen son Friedrich died in 1860, and all his relatives in Riga grieved his death.

Father's youngest brother, Gustav, owner of the estate Eckengraf in Courland, died in 1828 at the age of 34. He had been close to Father, and this friendship continued now with his wife, the widow Wilhelmine (née Vorkampff-Laue). She had no children but with tender love took care of her siblings' kids and she brought some of them up. After her husband had died, she stayed at the estate and then later sold it and moved to Friedrichstadt and then to Mitau. With her friendly heart and lively spirit, she was well-liked. Mother had an intimate friendship with her, and Father looked after all the business transactions for his sister-in-law. Often she travelled to Riga to stay for a few weeks at a time at the Boettichers' and they would visit her in Eckengraf. All the Boetticher children had great affection for Aunt Minna, and it felt like a tragedy for them as this relationship stopped after the sale of Eckengraf in 1844. A financial mishap had taken place, mainly the fault of her advisors, but it was blamed on Father. Even after things were cleared up, the friendship was over. Nevertheless, the children thought lovingly of this aunt and her characteristics. Strictness and kindness were paired wonderfully together in her. She was able to put her sharp judgment in a loving way so that one had to reflect on her words first to fully understand their meaning. Though she was friendly, the irony stung.

Later on, as Father got old, the friendship continued and she wrote to him.

Mitau, May 29, 1857

My dear true brother-in-law! I will travel to a spa in a foreign country on June 6. The winter has been poor, so I have to get away, but I won't leave before saying a hearty goodbye to you. You are probably living in Ebelshof and I would visit, but don't have the time. I will be in the "E's" house at my niece's on June 4 at 4:00 o'clock if you'd like to see me. It has been almost two years since I saw you, my good Boetticher, and heard little of you and besides Carl and Adele, none of your children care to see the old Aunt Minna, who is true to you all until she is dead.

Aunt Minna outlived our parents by many years but stayed in friendly contact with the Boetticher children right to the end.

To talk more about Father's more distant relatives is not of importance since the contact with them was somewhat loose. They did not live in Riga but in parts of Courland or inside the huge country or in St. Petersburg (Russia). Through many letters, Father was in contact with all of them. As some of them moved to Riga later on, they too experienced the hospitality at the Boettichers'. This was also the case if they ever travelled through Riga. Very often he helped financially those among his relatives who were not as fortunate as he was. The letters found are filled with their deepest thanks to this generous man.

Chapter 7

Contact with Other People

Here we need to talk about the people who were not relatives but good friends of the Boettichers.

One of them was Superintendent Daniel Gustav von Bergmann (born May 18, 1787; died April 21, 1848). He studied in Dorpat from 1806 to 1809 and then was adjunct at the Jesus Church in Riga; then he preached in the church in Bickern in 1819 and was deacon in the cathedral in Riga in 1838. He was the senior pastor in the same cathedral and from 1843 was senior pastor in St. Peter's Church in Riga. Bergmann combined a great knowledge of the arts and sciences. He was loved as a preacher and was a brilliant conversationalist and sometimes writer of poems. He belonged to the men of great modesty. His field did not teach politics but was used to create religious awakening, as a teacher to inspire, as a friend of the family, and to give comfort. His friendship with the parents must have been intimate, even by 1827. This we find in the letters he wrote on a trip through Germany.

At sad or happy times, confirmations or weddings, Bergmann helped with his poetic gift and poems to touch the hearts of all the people at the festivities. Many of his poems and writings have survived, and they show us his funny side and the close connection he had with the family. His death brought sadness to all.

One of the best friends of the family was the Bishop Dr. P. A. Poelchau. He too went to the university in Dorpat (1822 to 1824) and there became a close friend of the Boetticher son-in-law Dr. Fr. Sommer. Before 1843, he was archdeacon of the Petri Church in Riga, and when Bergmann became superintendent, he was the senior pastor at the cathedral (1848) and then the senior pastor and superintendent at the Petri Church, so for the second time, he took Bergmann's position. In later years, when Bergmann had died, Poelchau was the father confessor of the parents. In his ways, he was totally different from the former; solemn and dignified, he knew people well. A man of great speeches and master of the word, at Father's open graveside, he said, "He was a man of action, not of words." We have to mention here also that there is a close friendship between his children and the younger Boetticher kids right up to this day.

In the year 1874, when the youngest Boetticher son (Emil) had invited many friends and acquaintances to celebrate the opening of his new house, Pastor Poelchau was there to give a speech at the occasion. "The blessing of the parents builds houses for the children." At the end, he told everyone to raise his or her glass for a toast: "May the good spirit that used to live in the Boetticher house now move in here too and may respect to God and peace and good hospitality live on."

Not much later, he died at the age of 71. The blessing he gave the new house will never be forgotten by the owner.

Here are some of the names of people the Boettichers talked about. Foremost was Gotthard Dressler. Born in Libau, he retired early in life after a career as a merchant. Now a widower, he enjoyed the quiet lifestyle at Father's "El Dorado," Ebelshof, or he spent time with his friend Carl Boetticher. He was smart, had a sense of humor, and liked to read but lacked the drive to work hard like Father. So if he was traveling, Father looked after all the business for him in Riga. Dressler had a house built in Sannaxt and loved the country life there. From his letters to Father, we find him to be a very relaxed person. When some of his business in Riga showed major losses, he wrote to Father not to worry and not to give up on humankind. "The businessman, dear friend, will be subject like no other to fraud and losses and we would get otherwise too rich and lose touch with reality. This be our consolation." Of course, Father did not need such consolation but missed his friend a lot when he was away from Riga. Dressler occupied a small room on the upper floor of the Boetticher house and was part of the family.

Here are some names of people who came to visit sometimes as part of the wider circle of friends of the Boettichers: City Councillor

Bergengruen and the old Bergner, who kept Father company in his later years, and the friendly house doctor Bornhaupt. Everyone loved the visit of the old Dr. Hartmann, who helped Father by bringing him news and anecdotes. Father had great respect and admiration for Mayor G. D. Hernmarck. Both he and Otto Müller had guardianship of his younger sons. Hernmarck was born in Sweden and educated in Germany, but in his heart was a Riga patriot; he belonged among the most outstanding men that Riga had in that century. He was loved by everyone, and his communal service was outstanding. Otto Müller (born in Courland in 1813; died in Riga in 1867) was a close relative of Councillor Bergengruen and was brought up in his house. Already as a boy, he was often in our parents' house. A gifted person, smart, with a great knowledge of the law profession, he moved quickly up the ladder in Riga's city hall. As the mayor of the city, Otto Müller was known for his quick decisions and endless energy, which brought results. His patriotism and love of all humankind and his devotion to his friends, the young and old, made him the soul of the Riga Council when in 1861 the youngest son of the Boettichers' (Emil) started his career in the city hall of Riga. There he found friendly support from this man. He died much too early in life and was dearly missed by everyone.

Here we have to mention the civil servant Johann Anton Lange. Father became a friend of his when he served as councillor for two years. His engaging manner brought Mr. Lange many friends. He died in the year 1853.

Mr. Pfeil and Mr. Thilo both owned factories, and Father dealt with them. After Father had given up his business, he was still in contact with Mr. Thilo and appreciated him as a friend and businessman. He often asked him for his advice. His daughters Helene and Elise were well liked in the Boetticher house.

Chapter 8

Kruthen and Kokenhusen, The First Grandchild

When Ernst Kuehn was still pastor in Kruthen, the parents visited often. Lina had moved to Eckau in 1845 with her husband and welcomed her siblings and parents there on many occasions. Of course, the married children also travelled to Riga to live with their parents for days or weeks.

Near the end of January 1843, after recuperating from a long illness, Mother visited Kruthen and wrote to Riga on February 5, 1843, that the day before a daughter had been born. One can imagine how happy everyone was about this news, including the youngest ones. In her letter, Mother wrote, "What will Oscar and Emil say now knowing that they have become uncles?"

Of course, Mother stayed in Kruthen for the baptism. She was also the godmother of her grandchild. Father too made the trip, and in March 1843, they went back home together. Back in Riga, Mother wrote on March 25,

At 8:00 o'clock in the evening we were at the River Düna, which was free of ice just the day before. Mr. Haken, the land commissioner, was friendly enough to look after our carriage and with good weather like a summer evening we made it across in 15 minutes. Minna was surprised to see us so late in the evening. She had waited all day for us. The little boys were already in bed but wide awake from all the hugging and kisses they received, and Mayor Kuehn with his sister came up right away so we gave them the greetings we had brought along for them. The next day I inspected the rooms in our house and was very pleased with the way everything had been cleaned and made cozy. I thank God for looking after all my loved ones while I was away.

Mother was happy to be back in Riga and to be able to concentrate on her children back home. She had no plans to leave soon again but made plans to have her oldest daughter there in the summertime.

On April 14, 1843, she wrote, "The bad north wind is gone now and soon everything will be green. How much will I like Ebelshof with all the family at Witsun and the flowers everywhere."

Even though the roads were bad, the parents went to Kruthen in September 1843, and this time the two young boys came along. From the trip home on September 23, Mother wrote,

Oscar did not feel well and made a long face. Then as we had passed Windau things got better, and in the afternoon he and

Emil sang the song of the "speckled horse" for hours. The carriage driver took us to Neu-Autz and then with the same horses to Olai, where we arrived at 9:30. Here we had hot tea because it was bitter cold and got back home at 11 o'clock. Minna had set the table, but we all went to bed right away.

In February 1844, Mother spent time again in Kruthen. There she welcomed her second grandchild, this time a boy and an heir of the Kuehn family. She would have loved to stay there longer just to spoil the little ones with her love.

In the summer of 1844, Lina travelled to Ebelshof, this time with her two children. There the kids were the centre of attention, and the separation after a few weeks was very difficult. "How are the sweet children?" Mother wrote soon to Kruthen. "In the days after they left I thought I heard the voice of little Selma and other times the voice of Ernst, and I was really sad when the baby carriage was moved to the attic and the bedroom prepared for Ernestine and Minna again."

Chapter 9

Additions and Separation

As in the Kuehn family, later on the Pachts too had children, and Mother embraced them all with open arms. In these critical times, she spent weeks and months with her daughters to look after them, to watch the children, and to run the households. Her constitution was not very strong anymore, but she worked hard and "where her busy hands worked, everything happened quickly." But she still thought she was not doing enough. "Don't think I am odd," she wrote Father from Kokenhusen in July 1848 after the first son was born, "but I will feel a lot better after the care person has left, so that I can take care of the little one."

Being away for such a long time and so often was not easy for Mother. But it was her sense of duty to her daughters and her heart that drove her to help as much as possible. Here the letters helped to bridge the long separation. "As long as I get only good news from back home, I will stay strong and put all worries to the Father in heaven, who with his great kindness keeps away everything that scares and torments us. It is the worry about my house and its occupants and those I miss the most."

She was used to her many friends at home and felt isolated in Kokenhusen. Walks through the Bilsteinhof Forest, which she really enjoyed, could not make up for the loss of her friends. She wished that Father would buy the Bilsteinhof and use it for his summer residence.

In June 1848, Mother wrote from Kokenhusen, "Hermann made the suggestion to bring the boys over for a few weeks. I would look after them, and Oscar could enjoy the beautiful area around here." This wish came only partly true. Oscar had suffered since the end of the year from a long rheumatic problem with severe pain. He had to leave school, and Mother cared for him during the long time. She loved this son especially, but he was not able to come to Kokenhusen because he had to take spa treatments by doctor's orders. Now she welcomed her youngest son Emil.

She wrote Father,

I am happy that you sent Emil. It would have been so nice to have Oscar here, but we have to listen to the doctor and God help that he is back in shape soon. He is a good boy, and I hope that he will, with friendly behaviour, earn the love of the people around him in the new environment … I yearn to get home, it feels like I have been away for a year and not a month and with all my mental and physical power, I know where I belong.

Eight days later, on July 19, 1848, she wrote, "The yearning to get home gets stronger every day, and I try hard not to show my feelings to Amalie. Emil is happy here, goes for swims and does not work. Today he was catching fish. But all will be over soon and so I let him be."

Mother was home for a short while. In the fall, she was back in Eckau to help out, and only in October did she find rest in her own home.

In September and October 1848, she wrote letters from Eckau to Father.

I'd really like to know how our good Oscar is doing now with the change of climate. I hope you thought of Emil's birthday or did somebody remind you? I remember he wanted a stone and ore collection because the boys found this hobby playing in the Düna Estuary. Can you get something like that? I am happy to tell you that our Lina thrives better every day. The little girl does well with the nurse. If everything goes well, I want to be back by the end of next week. I don't know how to do it, but there will be a way. The thought of being back in my house makes me happy. Lina wants me to stay for the baptism, but I think you should make the trip here and I stay home. Pastor Grote told me about the terrible road at this time of year to Riga. Ernst will take me on Sunday from here to Balckenburg, and if you want to see me, my dear husband, you will have to send the carriage out. Please send the smallest, lightest equipage, the best would be a wicker carriage. With those, the chance of falling over on these bad roads is less likely. You know I am no hero when things go wrong, and with a loud scream, I would give my heart some extra air … I will see you soon and can hardly wait. I press you to my heart, your Emilie.

We followed Mother on her trips to her married daughters' and got to know the split feelings she had when she spent a large part of the year away from her home. At those times, the reliable Minna Lindenberg looked after the household in Riga and took care that Father and the younger siblings did not have to suffer too much while Mother was gone.

Chapter 10

Giving Up the Business, Father's Activities, From His Letters

Father gave up his business in the year 1844. Even so, he was still quite involved and busy with different guardianships and the management of his own land holdings and properties. All these he looked after with great care. In the earlier years, when he had worked too hard, his health had suffered, and now with less work, he complained of stress, something he had never done before. His cheerfulness during the early 1840s diminished, especially in the later years of his life. A man of energy and activity, he now was indecisive; all the fun that Father used to have was slowly lost. We have to mention that this change in his character happened over time, as he got older.

In the years 1843 and 1844, when he was still in good shape, he wrote letters to Kruthen, and on February 25, 1843, he wrote to Mother,

> What did you think of my youthful adventure, my dear wife, when I took the postal coach last Saturday at 1:00 for a six-and-a-half-hour drive on hard, frozen, bad roads for a joyride to Friedrichstadt. Twice, Minna (Father's sister-in-law née Vorkempff), invited me to celebrate Louis LXIV's birthday,

and without much thinking, I followed Minna's wish. At 7:30, I was at the shore of the River Düne across from Friedrichstadt. For a half hour, I used my loudest voice without result. The lazy men did not want to pick up this passenger with the boat, so I had to spend the night in a dirty inn and my worn-out, hurting bones did not even find a decent bed. On Sunday, I had recuperated already. At the old inn, the Laue, there were big congratulations, *thé dasant*, card playing and supper with champagne. We acted out some operas. Minna played the wife of the village innkeeper. Monday after lunch, I left but suffered even more because I got a terrible headache from the bumpy ride. For two days, I felt bad but now I am okay again. Our dear children and all occupants of the house are totally healthy and send greetings to you … All the gossip will probably be in the letters of the females written to you … Best regards to my old lady from her even older Carl.

On March 4, 1843, he wrote to his daughter,

You made me very happy with your nice letter, my dear Lina, that showed your well-being and how joyful you are, and now my heart is thankful towards God. As I see, the baptism will be on March 17 and you want me to bring Miss Müller and Lisinka along. Well yes, but who knows what kind of road we will have in eight days! I have no problems getting through myself … Your plans for the summer are great but don't forget I have them now in black and white. I will use all my power and see to it that you fulfill your promise to stay at Ebelshof … Be content, your child is not complete yet, now you have the joy to help it along at the slow development … I have to close, Wilcken is waiting for this letter … Greetings to …

On April 25, 1843, he wrote to his daughter,

I think often of you and your little child. God keep you healthy. In four weeks' time, I will meet you, my dear Lina, your child and my dear Kuehn. You have no idea how much we look forward to the good time we will have together. We hope to move off to Ebelshof in the next weeks. If it would not be so cold, we would have moved already since it is so beautiful to watch nature waking up.

Chapter 11

The Parsonage in Eckau, The Younger Families and the Old One, Father Getting Older, Kemmern and Ebelshof in the Year 1849

The move of the Kuehns (the oldest daughter) from Kruthen to Eckau was much welcomed by the parents. Father was not as mobile as he used to be and so the drive to the faraway Kruthen was arduous for him and he visited rarely. To reach the much closer Eckau was easier if the roads were good, and all the family members were attracted to its landscape, which was nicer than that of Ebelshof. The hospitality of the Pastor's wife, the friendly Pastor and his old father and his youthful wife, the happy bustle of the growing children—all this made the Eckau parsonage a good attraction. The whole family celebrated there New Year's Day and the birthday of the Pastor's wife on a regular basis, and there the boys spent much of their holidays. As the parents' house lost its occupants over the years, it got quieter. Everyone now met in Eckau, including Father, to be "among people."

Often the trip to Kokenhusen was made, but the distance from Riga was far and not easy to make, especially before the time of railroads. Father travelled not as often as the younger generation, and those were captivated by the spell of the romantic Perse Valley, the roar of the forest of the Bilstein Estate, and the view across the wide River Düna. Here Amalie and her hospitality made everyone feel welcome, just like in Eckau.

The marriage of the two older daughters brought great changes in the life of the parents. They wanted to spend their time with their children and not at home with their many friends and acquaintances. As life at home got quieter, it got livelier at the daughters'. The happy atmosphere in the parents' house that had dominated had also changed since Father's had health deteriorated. The old rheumatic pain was back, and the high blood pressure in his head made his life miserable. Doctor Bornhaupt ordered spa treatments at the Kemmern Bath, and Father moved there with the two younger boys in June 1849. Oscar had bad rheumatism in 1847. The spa in Kemmern in 1848 had helped him a lot, so a second stay there was recommended. Emil came along just for company. They also met Miss Müller there. She had left the Boettichers' in the meantime. The boys liked having Father's favorite horse along. In the mornings, it had to stand in the sulfuric water to strengthen its legs, and in the afternoon, the boys went riding with it.

Father's health improved among interesting people. The boys had a really good time there. Mother managed Ebelshof during that time and proved that no job was too difficult for her. Theodor, who was an apprentice at the Strauss firm and the youngest daughter,

Lisinka, should have been staying in Ebelshof with her, but the happy beach life in Dubbeln with the parties and dances had more to offer than the quiet of Ebelshof. Theodor, known to be a good rider and dancer, often took his fast horse to the beach resort five kilometres away where the young ladies much appreciated him as a dancer. He also acted as a chaperone for his sister Lisinka, who was staying with the Hernmarck family in Dubbeln to enjoy all the activities there.

At this time, Mother invited many friends to stay with her at Ebelshof sometimes for weeks. To look after her health, she made the daily trip to Riga to swim in the cold water of the River Düna. "As we old folks trying to stay in shape, maybe our youth will be back!" she wrote Father with regard to his and her self-prescribed treatment. She had a lot of fun during a trip she made with her daughter and her husband from Eckau in the summer of 1849 to Kemmern and the beach resorts to visit Father, the boys and friends. Today, by train, it is an easy trip. At that time, it was an arduous journey. But why have horses in the stable? They used the old carriage, which had seen a lot during the trips of 1840 and 1841. Four strong horses pulled it through the deep sand. There was a happy reunion in Kemmern. Then on the way back, they had a visit in Karlsbad with the Pfeil family and in Dubbeln a visit at the Hernmarcks'. They had another at the relatives' von Radetzky-Mikulicz and a third at Pastor Hellman's. Late in the evening, she was back in Ebelshof. From there, Mother wrote the next day to Father how nice the day had been and how the horses had gotten a good exercise also.

Chapter 12

Engagements of Carl and Friedrich and Their Marriages, The Daughters-in-Law: Adele and Eugenie

At that time, Mother was still very active, whereas Father rarely and seldom left the house. The spa in Kemmern did not help him with his ailments. He decided on the advice of the doctor to make a spa trip in 1850 to a foreign country. But before we get there, we have to report on two important happenings in the family during the year 1849. We let Mother talk about one of the happenings in a letter to her daughter Amalie on November 4, 1849.

> Since we saw each other (end of October), only a short time has passed but things can change quickly. Why should I start with long introductions? I call you with a happy heart: Carl is engaged to Adele Baumgarten, a friendly, lovely girl, who, in the short time we have known her, has won all our hearts. We had no idea that Carl would get married so quickly, but living in the country alone is probably the reason. We were surprised when Carl showed up on Saturday. The old Papa looked a bit unhappy because he thought the estate (in Pommusch) would suffer in his absence. We had no clue that Carl came to inform us of his plans, but he was restless and

we knew that something was on his mind. Monday morning, he told us he got the "yes" from his Adele on Saturday. Even with all the rush and surprise, I promised to receive Adele as a daughter. Father was not too happy and said everything was done too quickly and not thought through. But Carl's heart was too happy, so he shrugged off Father's reservations and was allowed to introduce his bride. In the evening, we received the young people lovingly and now I feel as if I have known Adele for a long time already. It would be impossible to look into her open face without loving her.

Adele's Father is an organist in Windau, a respected and good man. With ten children, his daughter lacks in a better education, but she is still young and Carl can teach her in quiet hours by reading good books and so on. We see Adele every day. Carl does not want to wait until the new house in Pommusch is ready but would like to get married by Christmas. It is possible to fix up rooms in the old house in the meantime. Father wants Adele to take music lessons now so she is able to sing along. Her singing voice is alto and matches very well with Carl's voice, and I'm sure we will have many nice hours singing and making music. This morning, Carl drove back to Pommusch.

The engagement of the oldest son brought new life into the parents' house. The new bride, even though she was different in some ways from the daughters of the house, quickly won everyone's heart, including the old father, who had fun recognizing her as a daughter. On February 5, 1850, the wedding was held, and the young couple moved to Pommusch. Early on, Adele found plenty of opportunity to show her efficiency and competence. A few months had passed since the wedding. During this time, Carl was busy erecting new structures; now he had the company of his young wife. Just as the distillery built in a remodeled house on the property was completed, it was destroyed by fire, and in a short time, all was gone and what had cost a lot of time, effort and money. And as if this was not enough, the mental and physical stress to fight the fire was too much for Carl's constitution. For a long time after, a rheumatic paralysis made it impossible for him to move or speak.

"God is testing us," Mother wrote from Pommusch on April 21, 1850, where she had gone immediately after the accident. "Let's not give up, but carry on with courage. With great patience Adele takes care of her husband and it looks like God has sent this angel to console him."

By the summer of 1850, Carl was healthy again because of the care of Adele and the spa treatments, which acted like a miracle in Kemmern.

Besides the engagement of Carl, another important family event happened during the year 1849. This time the news came from the faraway Saxony, and it was not a letter by Mother but from the son Friedrich. As we said before, he started his education in agriculture at the institute of Director E. Stoeckhardt in Brösa near Bautzen in 1849. From there, he wrote to his parents on June 7,

> During the four weeks I am here, I got to know the women of this household well. They, the mother-in-law, the wife and sister of the owner are almost as close to me as Mother and sisters. I will be sorry to leave these nice people. I will move on in four weeks' time ...

A letter sent from Dresden August 6 showed that he had visited the Schwabe family in Weimar and had used his holiday to see München, Zürich and Strassburg. He also visited Heidelberg, Stuttgart, and Hohenheim and on his way back took the steamship on the River Rhine to Düsseldorf. From Hannover, he got back to Saxony. From Brösa, he wrote to his parents on September 1, 1849:

> When I moved here I had no idea that I would find the love of my life and it was tough to leave for the trip. I've known her for four months now, and we spend all our free time together. We are happy and in love. Eugenie is from a long line of preachers: her deceased father, grandfather and great-grandfather were pastors, and also her mother's father and

grandfather had the same profession. The Pastor's wife, Mrs. Mitschke, Eugenie's mother and the wife of Director Stoeckhardt, Eugenie's older sister, are great women and I am happy to call them Mother and Sister. I respect Director Stoeckhardt as an excellent agriculturist and what is of even greater value, as a person.

Eugenie is a young woman with education, modest and dignified and beautiful. Her education was done by the parents: her father taught her science, music and the Italian language; her mother all the chores of a good housewife. Eugenie is quite busy and gets up at four o'clock in the morning to help her mother. The workload is endless for them, but they stay away from all materialism. Eugenie is two years younger than I am. She can be serious and still happy. She does not talk much, and her disposition is deep ... I have been a farmer now for the past year and would really like to be the owner of a farm one hour away from Brösa. There is a great opportunity to buy this place with a nice house, including the inventory, for about 26000 thaler ... Please give me the means if at all possible to buy this place. It would complete my happiness.

The parents gave their consent to Friedrich's marriage even though it meant him staying in faraway Germany and becoming an agriculturist. For both parents, losing a son that way was very difficult. But Friedrich was determined to stay and his bride would not have left her homeland either. The purchase of the knight's manor that Friedrich had mentioned in his letter took place on April 6, 1850. From May 1850, he managed his new estate, and on August 1, 1850, he married Eugenie Mitschke and moved with her to Zschillichau.

Friedrich's bride had at first contact with his parents only with her letters. Theodor, who visited his brother in Brösa in March 1850, was the first member of the family to meet Friedrich's bride personally. Close-knit, as all the Boettichers were, they now had the desire to meet Eugenie. This chance came up for Father, who, by doctor's orders, was to take a trip to Germany for a treatment at Franzenbad (a spa) to improve his health.

Chapter 13

Father's Last Trip to a Foreign Country, Life in Bigaunzeem

In May 1850, Father left Riga with his daughter Lisinka, his adopted daughter Minna, and a friend of his daughter's Miss Emma Hahr. He took a ship to Lübeck (Germany) and from there travelled to Hamburg and further to Dresden and then to visit Friedrich in Zschillichau and his bride in Brösa.

The letters that Father and the siblings wrote from this trip have not survived. Any information we have is from letters Father received from home. We know that the travellers, after the spa treatment in Franzen, saw Vienna, the Alps, Austria, Tyrol, and Switzerland and were back in Riga in September. In the meantime, Mother managed her homes in Riga and in Ebelshof and then for some weeks in the summer, enjoyed a holiday with her children and grandchildren not far from Kemmern in a beach house in Bigaunzeem. In the fall, she went to Kokenhusen to welcome a new grandchild. She would have loved to be on the trip with Father to meet the new daughter-in-law. "Thank God that you feel so strong," she wrote to Father in Dresden on May 26, 1850, "and are able to walk hard with the boys; just don't overdo it on your outings. There is no need to rush … I wish I could go with you to Zschillichau; that would be nice. Bring greetings to our son and his wife. May the luck for a good family life be with them and this not be built on sand, then the grace from above will come." A few days later, she wrote,

I loved Minna's report from the nice visit to Hamburg and the speedy trip to Leipzig, so for a moment, when reading these lines, I wanted the same enjoyment; but then here (in Ebelshof) it is nice too with the children and friends and when you are all back home the lamp on the sofa table will shine for us all. I hope the kids will tell me about the adventures of their tour. I can hardly wait to get a letter from Dresden and hope it is a detailed report. I always think that the wedding of Friedrich should be on his birthday, June 11, during your stay there. To be in your midst for one hour is my heart's desire but unfortunately not possible!

In June 1850, Carl and his young wife had moved to Kemmern. Shortly after, Mother and her crew were in Bigaunzeem. We read about the life there in a letter written by their son-in-law Ernst Kuehn on July 1, 1850, to Father.

Just like you, I left all work behind and made a journey, only my goals were smaller; after only two days we arrived at our destiny in Bigaunzeem on the Bay of Riga, close to the entry to Kemmern. Nature here at the beach is beautiful, but it cannot be compared with what the arts and the people offer where you are. From far away I send greetings to all of you and may God bless the young couple on their journey through married life! May God be with them at all times!

We arrived here at the beach on June 27. Our little house is nice—and what is more important, it is dry and healthy. But sand is everywhere, in front, behind and this is good in a way; the children can play all day without supervision on the beach. Your grandson loves it. The shoes were off at the first, because they were wet. He walks barefoot into the sea and tries to catch fish. This makes him happy, and I am glad to have such a bright lad and think even the strictest grandfather would have fun with him. Not all the members of our group have arrived yet. Mother with Sophie Lindenberg and I and my four oldest children are here at this moment. Within the next days, we expect Malchen and her family, Oscar and Emil, who stayed in Kokenhusen for a few days, my sister Pauline and Pauze from Bauske. Then our colony is complete and every spot taken. Kemmern is close and that is good. I kept my carriage here and so we can go and see Carl and Adele daily. Pacht will also be there. About Carl, I can give you good news, dear Father. He can walk without a cane, has no pain and even danced; his hand has not yet the old power … it is expected that he will leave Kemmern completely healed. Emotionally he is much better, happy and lively; he takes part in all activities. Today we will see him here on the beach where the bachelors K. plan a coffee and bathing party and Adele and Louise Bornhapt will be the hostesses. We too are invited.

It is late in the evening! The party was a real success. The nice music made the old and the young dance. Adele has won the hearts of the Kemmern men and is well respected by all. The planned water tour had to be canceled because of strong winds. Now friendly greetings, my dear Father! With all the joyful time you are having, think of us too. May God keep you happy and healthy and may he bring you and the sisters back home this way. Give Friedrich and Eugenie my brotherly blessings and may God keep you, dear Father.

Mother was happy too with life near the beach. There were 19 people under one roof, and if things got a bit crazy at times, it was Mother who enjoyed all the bustling activity the most.

It was always a celebration if news arrived from a foreign country. Then the whole colony gathered around and someone had to read aloud. Surrounded by young people and the different environment, Father had found his old physical and mental strength. Mother was really worried that he would do too much and warned him about forceful marches by day or driving by night. She wrote,

Dear little man, I beg you to remember that you are 68 years old and keep this in mind not to make strenuous trips and go mountain climbing. Rather see less but enjoy it more. Also take the land route back; it would be a lot more reassuring for me if you are not out at sea in the end of September.

Mother disliked staying in larger cities for too long and thought they should have been avoided more. "Large cities offer a lot in the fields of art and culture, but the beautiful mountains, valleys and lakes, talk in a different way to the hearts of the people, for everyone who knows God's power, grace and wisdom."

Good news not only arrived in Bigaunzeem and later on in Ebelshof from the travellers, but also Father's excellent reports from back home. Carl was healthy; Oscar showed no signs of his previous ailments, and all had a wonderfully refreshing time at the beach; a great summer brought a very good harvest in Pommusch and Ebelshof. On August 27, another grandson was born in Kokenhusen and the joy at home was heightened by the good results that Pacht had at the spa in Kemmern. In short, luck and joy was felt on both sides. As Father had embraced his new daughter-in-law in Germany, so the other daughter-in-law at home in Pommusch had won Mother's heart completely.

August was almost over, and it was time for Father and his two daughters to get home. Mother had promised to travel to Kokenhusen to see Amalie. She took the road past Engelhardshof and Siggund to visit her two youngest at the former to celebrate the birthday of Oscar and to stay with the "good Albanus" for the day. She was afraid she would miss the travellers as they arrived back in Riga. Amalie liked Mother's company very much, so she wrote to Father not to rush but to enjoy and take in all the beauty. Then she said,

> You asked me what you could bring along. To buy big expensive gifts is out of the question. To prove that someone had thought of another person when far away by buying gifts is not important. I only have one request; Oscar's birthday is in a few days, and I would like him to have a simple silver watch, one you can get for 12 to 14 thalers. Emil's birthday is on October 1. Do you want to buy him one too, or shall we wait another year? They are good boys, and if God will take care of them for us, we will have great joy.

Chapter 14

Homecoming, Engagement of Elise, The Brother-in-Law Theodor and His First Wife, Engagement and Marriage of Minna Lindenberg, Marriage of Elise

In October 1850, the travellers were back home and Mother too was back from Kokenhusen. To welcome Father and the sisters, the boys were brought over from Engelhardtshof, and not only Oscar, but also little Emil, got a watch from Father.

The boys went back for schooling but in all likelihood, would rather have stayed home with their parents. Here everything looked so joyful. As always in the evening, the lamp on the table before the red sofa was burning. Everyone sat together with the members of the family and guests to talk about the interesting experiences, the beautiful countries, and the arts they had seen. More often than previously, among the guests, a man showed up who belonged to the wider circle of the relatives but now showed a special interest in what the youngest daughter Lisinka (Elise) had to say. Did she not also listen to every word he said? Did her face not show her fascination with his quick remarks, his sharp thinking, and his great knowledge? Shortly after her return from the trip, Lisinka wrote to her close brother-in-law in Kokenhusen,

My dear Hermann, and you, my good, dear Malchen! I bring you happy news. I am a bride! … My heart jumps for joy. Oh God I am so happy. I can't find the words to express my feelings. Celebrate with me. To be loved by this man is heaven on earth … I have loved Theodor for a long time and on the trip in Germany I thought of him all the time, which gave me many gloomy hours but also many happy ones. Hermann, I hope you are not mad at me because I became a bride so quickly and without your consent. But I did not even ask the parents for their okay. I took no time to think; my heart was beating for him for a long time. My dear brother-in-law, I ask for respect; I tell you, I'm not only a bride but also a mother of a small son, who gave me the keys to the house yesterday.

The year 1850 ended with Lisinka being the bride of Theodor Boetticher, and as this event was celebrated, Minna Lindenberg wrote to her sister Lina in Eckau, "I am a happy bride. On New Year's Day, I will introduce him to you and the other family members. Please receive him with love! This I beg you, your Minna." The man she was talking about was highly respected and much loved by the Boetticher family—Dietrich von Rodde, a man who was loved and honoured all his life and at whose side Minna found great happiness.

The groom of Elise, Carl Johann Theodor von Boetticher, was the son of the lawyer Philipp Boetticher in Mitau, born September 28, 1819. From 1836 to 1841, he studied philology and then law in Dorpat, took one semester in Königsberg, and after finishing made a trip through Germany and then was employed as secretary at the Courland High Court. Since 1848, he had lived in Riga. There he was first secretary at the Office of the General Governor and in 1853 became councillor at the court from where he resigned in 1865 for health reasons. Theodor had a friendly relationship with the Boettichers even before he moved to Riga. This we have seen from a number of letters he had written to Father.

As we said before, Theodor Boetticher had settled in Riga 1848 with his young wife Marie. All the Riga relatives welcomed her with open arms. Her winning manner enchanted all. She was married to Theodor for less than five years and gave birth to three children. A few days after she gave birth to the youngest, she died on March 20, 1849. All the children were sick with scarlet fever. The two oldest died, and only the youngest was saved. At the time when Theodor Boetticher lost almost all of his family, he was 30 years old. The many interests, the mental work, and the friendship of the men among the Riga relatives helped him survive his great loss.

With Lisinka's love for the ideal world, this man of education and high spirit, someone who did not fit the average stereotype, now fascinated her. He too found her to be special. She may not have possessed the beauty of his first wife, but she had a very loving heart and a deep disposition and brought joy to everyone around her.

In the letter to her brother-in-law Hermann Pacht, we read about her jubilation. Her parents and siblings too were happy for her and her future at the side of this man. Everyone liked the fact that Lisinka would stay in Riga. The wedding was celebrated on April 12, 1851, and she moved with her husband and stepson into an apartment just ten minutes from her parents' house. There they lived in five small rooms on the third floor of the Münder house. Her love for art showed in every room, and she surrounded herself with beautiful decorations.

The relatives of her husband, his mother and his sisters and sister-in-law, not only welcomed Lisinka but also loved and adored her. She returned this love to all and especially to her stepson. To her own parents, she was a ray of the sun that brought them light during the darker days.

At the beginning of 1851, Minna too left her parents' house. After the wedding, she lived in Riga and felt closely connected to the family with whom she had spent her youth. Her husband was loved by her father and treated like a son and by her foster siblings like a brother.

Chapter 15

Quiet Days, Miss Müller, Father's Failing Health, Oscar's Health

After the daughters had left their parents, Mother hired the former governess, Miss Müller, as a companion and to read to them. But the spell of the youth and former happy times were gone and so was the charming way of this lady. Her tone was different now, as Mother was used to being around Lisinka and Minna. It was good for the old folks to have both of them and the husbands close by, and they were welcome guests in the big house and filled it with young life.

The weekdays went by monotonously and quietly, but on Sundays, the dining room table was extended. Around it not only the daughters with their husbands gathered but also some of the old friends of the parents and new friends and relatives of the son-in-law Theodor. Among them were his brothers-in-law von Tornauw and von Radetzky-Mikulicz; his sisters Clara and Helene; and sometimes his friends Otto Müller, Faltin, Schütz, and others. Father loved this diversion when his guests felt comfortable, and Mother liked to share the best the house had to offer.

In the meantime, Father's health declined. He slowly got weaker, and this made writing difficult and also working. Looking after Ebelshof became a chore and to get rid of it, he rented the farm to someone. Now he watched as his darling, where he had spent freely over many years more time and money than he ever got back, was abused by the new businessman, who tried to make a healthy profit. So the rental contract was canceled soon after and a reliable manager put in place.

Even though Father had lost interest in managing his little estate Ebelshof, he very much enjoyed reading about the progress and success his sons had in Pommusch and Zschillichau. He studied the detailed reports and plans in the area of agriculture and was happy to read how enthusiastically Friedrich especially was engaged in this field. He also enjoyed the fact that Theodor had changed his mind after a longer stay in England to become a merchant and now had doubts. He had given up the idea of trying his luck in the New World and come back to be a farmer also.

In the year 1851, Oscar had to move back home with his parents. After he had measles, he had gotten eye problems, which lasted for a long time, and under these circumstances, schooling at the institute was impossible. For weeks and months, he had to stay in a darkened room, and as his suffering eased a little, he still had to be very careful. For him and for Mother, who took great care of him, this was an extremely difficult time. During this time of adversity and sorrow, a close relationship formed between Mother and son, one of friendship and trust like no other son had experienced. In the many letters that Oscar received from Mother when he was living in Germany, we can feel her motherly heart. We also read about her exact experience during her last years.

During the time of his eye problems, while he was living at home, there was also a friend of his youth, Antonie Knieriem, living at his parents' house. She later became the wife of Pastor Stender and was now in Riga to finish her education. Usually the oldest grandchild from Eckau, Lina's daughter Selma, lived with our parents at that time. Antonie looked after the eye patient, and together, they studied history and geography; she told him the names and dates, and he would try to remember them. Oscar, who was very gifted musically, was not allowed to read sheet music. So he played the piano just by ear and kept this way of reproducing music all through his life.

Chapter 16

Mother's Last Trip, Zschillichau, Friedrich and Eugenie, The Old Mrs. Schwabe

Oscar with his reoccurring eye problems needed an occupation where his eyes were not overused. For now, he was to attend the Klügmann Business School in Lübeck, Germany. Mother took him there and then made two trips to Zschillichau and other places. "If one travels like me," Mother wrote about this trip, "I will use my time as best as possible." Here are some excerpts that are of interest to us.

Berlin, June 17, 1853

The travel by ship to Swinemünde was not to my liking and my decision right then was to go back by a land route. Stettin is a busy place with nice parks between the old fortress walls. We drove to an entertainment district called "Elysium" and listened to the music of the summer theatre. Like everywhere else in Germany, the families sit with their beer and enjoy the music (even though it's not always the best) but they all look happy and content. Oscar was pleased to meet Mr. Struck, who had just left Riga. Here was one acquaintance among all the strangers, and with this joyful surprise, we all went to a restaurant and ordered steak. Last night we heard "The White Lady." The theatre is a beautiful new building, nicely decorated, and I wish Riga had one like it. The very well known tenor Roger from the opera in Paris is guest singer now in Stettin in the role of Georg Braun. Oscar, who had never seen this opera, was very enthusiastic about the music and the performance.

I am sitting now in my room in the Hotel Brandenburg. The weather is overcast and I don't know if I will be able to go outside. It would be sad if it rains all the time when we visit Berlin.

Zschillichau July 7–19, 1853

We took the route past Magdeburg, Halle and Leipzig and then to Dresden, where we had been expected for a long time and now we arrived in Zschillichau on July 16 at our children's. Minna Boetticher, who had been in Dresden a few days before me, definitely wanted to see Friedrich and meet Eugenie and as she met the Pastor's wife, Mrs. Mitschke said: "I am not the mother!" From that day on, all the relatives expected us daily. With the Baehrs, Minna Kyber and Minna Boetticher, we had a pleasant day in Dresden. Here in the country everything is so quiet after visiting the cities with the many people at the train ... The area around Bautzen is lovely. The view from here towards the Bautzen Mountains is picturesque, I find, and I'm surprised about the beautiful fields and meadows that Friedrich has and the care he takes to keep everything in great shape and the way he enjoys his properties. That he wants to sell everything is painful for me, when he loves it so much and still ...

After he has sold his estate, Friedrich's plan is to move to Leipzig. Here he wants to learn the business of book merchant at the book dealer R. and get involved to do editorial work at the paper ... and to get the exact knowledge about the publisher and commission business dealing with books. Anyway, he wants to own a bookshop in the city, and Eugenie is happy to go where he is going to settle. I will ask Friedrich to think it over and not to rush selling this beautiful farm.

Little Marie [Friedrich's daughter] is a pale, blond child, and very hard to get to know. I have tried my best with her. But she is very close and friendly to her parents and her grandmother (Mitschke). She speaks a few words and is outside in the fresh air. Eugenie spends a lot of time in her kitchen, which I think is not necessary with her small family. I would really like to take Eugenie and Friedrich along on the tour through the Saxon Switzerland, but she has problems walking the hills and he has no time, as the harvest has just started. So I will leave next Sunday, the 24th, for Dresden, then take two days for the excursions to Tharand and Bastei and from there make my way past Weimar to Kassel. I still have the energy to enjoy all the beauty that God has created in this world and so I will, together with my dear Oscar, see all the splendor to come back home rich with memories and then spend my energy for all my loved ones …

Weimar 18–30, July 1853

We left Zschillichau on July 20. Friedrich came along with us to Bautzen. The children took great care of me, and I really like Eugenie. It would be nice to have these children closer to home. On the 26th, we made our tour to the Bastion. Mr. Baehr was our guide. We had an enjoyable day together. I still remembered the tour across the Winterberge from previous times, and I was tired, so I turned back from the Rathe Forest in the evening with Baehr and left Oscar with other young men to hike their way further to Hohenstein, from where they got back the next evening very animated and happy about all the things they had seen.

The day before yesterday we arrived here in Weimar and are staying in the Hotel de Russie. I was really happy to see the nice

Kuhns and the old Mrs. Schwabe and be welcomed by them as in previous times. Yesterday noon we had to stay with them and we exchanged all the news about our lives … Yesterday we went to the castle to see the beautiful rooms of Schiller and Goethe with their fresco and Oscar checked out Schiller's apartment. Mrs. Schwabe's three grandsons showed us the gardens of the castle, and then Oscar wanted to visit the Goethe house.

Eisenach, July 30, 1853

I was not able to finish the letter from Weimar because the friendly Mrs. Kuhn walked in to pick me up to go to their Mother (Mrs. Schwabe). From there the horse carriage was to take us to the train. The old lady Schwabe had made cake and sandwiches and the wine was waiting, so hungry or not we had to eat and drink a toast to the happy return. If we don't meet here again, later on we will all meet where there is no more separation. It is so nice if one is far from home with all the strangers to find a heart that beats for us. And I am sure these nice people love you too since you were so close to the old Mr. Schwabe.

We arrived here in Eisenach at noon and then made the tour through the Marien Valley, the Landgrafen Gorge, the Anna Valley, the Dragon Valley, High Sun, Hörsel and Dragonstein. Everywhere beautiful views far away and closer to the Wartburg ... At the Wartburg, we could not see far, as it had become overcast and still it was nice to know one was surrounded by a great past ... Tomorrow we leave for Kassel and from there to Frankfurt and Mainz. How is Emil? He must write and tell me all about the relatives. I also want news about our people ... Saxony's countryside is beautiful with the well-established fields and orchards everywhere. We could change a lot back home with more time and care to prepare the soil. In a few weeks, I am back with you all. Oh how I wish to find you all happy and healthy, especially you, my dear husband. Don't work too hard or write much. Let Steffenhagen do the work for you. I'm sure he will find out quickly how you want the work done.

Chapter 17

Cholera in Riga, Mother's Speedy Return, Theodor in Arzen, Friedrich Back Home Living in His Parents' House

The news that arrived from Riga for the travellers was very unsettling. Cholera had started again and brought fear to all. Father did not feel well and was often lonely; he was yearning for Mother. The travel program was therefore simplified and shortened. She went from Eisenach to Kassel, Frankfurt, and Mainz and then took a Rhine tour to Cologne and back to Mainz. From there, Mother took the shortest way to visit Zschillichau for the second time, and after she had taken Oscar to Lübeck, against her former decision, took the ship back home. In the first half of August, she was back in Ebelshof.

In the meantime, Father had felt lonesome. In Birkenruh, Emil had finished his exam before Johanni (June 21) and spent some time with his sisters Lisa and Lisinka, who with their families took holidays at the Wirgen Inn near Libau. So in Ebelshof only Miss Müller looked after Father, and for a few days, Theodor stayed over. He had just taken over the Estate Arzen but in the meantime as his house was being built lived there in Mesothen. Even though it brought great joy to Father to help his sons establish themselves in their new businesses and their own households, the long separation from them was hard for his overall mood. The older he got, the more he felt neglected by the people around him. When he was 70 years old, the strong power had left him and this bothered him a lot; things that were previously easy tormented and worried him. Under these circumstances, it is understandable that Mother broke off her trip, which was originally planned to be longer, to get home quickly. Friedrich too after he had sold his estate in Zschillichau in August 1853 hurried home to Riga where he arrived with his wife and daughter Marie on September 30. The parents welcomed him with open arms and were very happy.

Up to this time, Friedrich had lived as a Russian subject in Germany. Now the time for which he was allowed to live away from his homeland had run out. His future was to be decided in Riga. The parents did not want him to immigrate. They loved to have all the children close by. Also they were sure that it was easier to own a farm in Latvia than in Germany and would do anything to help Friedrich get an estate there. Yet he was not sure if he wanted to live in the country back home; it was not the ideal plan for him. He would rather own a bookshop in Riga, but this was not a lucrative business to be in at that time. Also, his wife missed her Saxonian homeland too much to make the separation permanent, and Friedrich did not like living there that much, which had made him move to Germany in the first place.

Being back in Riga must have made him battle hard for a decision, but the outcome was predictable. In one way, the love of his parents made him want to stay, but the drive to establish himself in a business of his liking, one that felt right, made him immigrate. After living in his parents' house for six months, he left the old homeland, and after this decision, he never came back.

Father was really happy to have one of his sons at home, and Friedrich did everything possible to cheer him up. He spent a lot of time, patience, and energy on his interests. It was not the solving of difficult business, but small things that had to be done carefully to please the nature of this old man. Mother admired the patience and friendliness of this true helper, but she also knew that he was not happy doing this and the drive to start a new life must have been stronger every day.

Friedrich's wife, Eugenie, had a hard time settling down. She found everything different in the new country, painfully different, and it would have been easier for her if she had run her own household. Now she was a guest in her in-laws' house. Still even with all the love she received from them, they could never replace her own relatives. The hope of seeing them the next summer made life a little easier, even though Friedrich had not made up his mind at this time. At this difficult time, her son Walter was born on November 29, 1853, in Riga. We read about this event and many others in the letters that Mother wrote to Oscar and other happenings from the parents' house and family.

Chapter 18

Mother's Letters to Oscar

Even though some people had moved far away, Mother always felt the need to stay in close contact with them by writing many letters, and after Oscar had left, it was mainly he who received her correspondence.

She wrote on December 15, 1853:

When you get these lines, you will not be among your parents and siblings, but still with good, friendly people who mean well and spend Christmas with you. We, the ones far away, share your joy and our spirit is close. And to show our love that is so richly given this time of year, we sent this bank draft to buy anything that is useful and makes you happy … The way I know you, you would rather buy books than golden trumpery; a little chain on the vest is nice to look at, but nothing more than good for the eye, whereas a literary work will give you constant enjoyment. But do as you like, and we know our Oscar will make the right choice.

On November 29, a grandson was born, who looks cheerful into the world. Eugenie is well and sends her greetings to you. She had hoped to invite you for Christmas to her house, but things worked out differently than we had thought a few months ago. It seems Eugenie has settled in now, but Friedrich has not. His mind is not made up about his future business adventure.

You, my dear Oscar, I beg you, be modest and undemanding; forgive the failings of others and follow the goal that you have set for your future occupation with all energy.

Today your siblings who were here to buy Christmas gifts are driving home. Lina bought many things for her full house, and Carl, who has to buy gifts for his wife and children, also must have spent some extra rubles for other people in his life. Theodor wants to decorate his own tree and invite the Pommusch children and the children of his landlady Treuland, but on the 24th, he will be celebrating with us. May God give us a happy and peaceful celebration! And may a festive mood enter everyone's heart. I pray for that.

Pacht was here eight days ago just for 24 hours, and I don't know how he made this trip in the terrible weather. Amalie is healthy and very busy with her four boys. For those little fellows, I bought a number of things, but Amalie will not be happy about the drum that Hans is supposed to get. In about 14 days, Emil will be here with us. He did not even write yet so I don't know if he got my last letter. I expect a letter from you at Christmas.

Riga, December 30, 1853

Thank you, my dear Oscar, for your letter, which I got the Sunday before Christmas at the same time as Minna with her husband and children was here for the baptism of the grandson. His name is Walter. He is a healthy child we all like very much. Eugenie is busy with her children and stays often in her room where it is warmer than in our larger rooms. It is very cold outside right now. The Christmas table was decorated again with many gifts accompanied by funny verses in the form of riddles that each person had to solve. I will make an exception and not go to Eckau tomorrow; I will visit the children a few weeks later and stay for a while. We thought about you, my dear son, when the Christmas tree was lit and as I attended church on Christmas Day. It was a consolation to know that you, too, said a prayer at the same hour at church to the giver of all the good. May God bless you in the New Year and be with you and give you the power to all good, so we have a happy reunion.

Riga, January 11, 1854.

Today Emil left us, he probably will be back home in his summer holidays. Right after Easter, the religious instructions begin in Wolmar; a few other boys of the school will also attend. I am happy that Walter will be teaching ... Emil looks better now than in the springtime, and he is almost as tall as Friedrich. He is more serious but can be very joyful.

Here we wait of the things to come, a certain suspense. God give that the political uncertainty will be resolved in a peaceful way, even though we don't expect any Turks here. Circumstances could change.

Father did not mind the drive to Eckau and maybe this will encourage him to make the much longer trip to Kokenhusen. Amalie would really like that because of all the siblings she gets the least visitors. I hope the roads will be better soon so I can visit all the children in the country.

Riga, February 1854

I took two weeks to see the children, and I had a good time. Whereas Father and the siblings here had seen them early in the New Year, I was at home to be with Eugenie. Then I was in Eckau for four days and in Pommusch for three days, saw Theodor in his nice new apartment, and with Adele and Theodor, we went to Kokenhusen. Amalie was surprised and very happy to see us, and we stayed four days. Adele saw Kokenhusen for the first time and enjoyed the winter scenery. A drive through the beautiful Bilsteinhof Forest to the Düna (River Daugava) and another one to the estate and to the church were really nice trips. Adele regretted not seeing all the beauty in the summertime where everything looks even nicer.

It is funny how the characters of the grandchildren are so very different. How they each develop is remarkable. Selma and Ernst (Eckau) with three other boys get schooling by a house teacher. They are in the early stages of learning and have a hard time. The children in Pommusch are well behaved. The little girl (15 months) is very smart; not only does she speak everything, but also answers all questions. Hans (Kokenhusen) is growing up fast; the two younger brothers, Walter and Hermann, play well together with him.

Little Minna from Eckau has been living with us for the last eight days; she is a friendly, affectionate child … Eugenie and Friedrich still do not feel at home here; the talk is that he wants to look for a place to live in Saxony. She is often sad and in tears, homesick. In the beginning, Friedrich looked after the paperwork and letters for Father, but now Father took back this job. You know how difficult he is in such matters.

Riga, March 8, 1854

Father was very happy about your dear letter and thanks you for the nice wishes on his birthday. Thank God he is still around for us! Even though he is sometimes tired and exhausted, he suffers no bad health problems like many people 72 years old. With our children living out of town, only the two sons-in-law were here for his birthday. So in the morning, we had not that many voices to sing a choral. Therefore, we waited until Father was dressed and the guests had congratulated him to sing together the nice choral "How Big Is the Almighty's Kindness." For lunch, some more old friends showed up and the day ended very pleasantly.

The overall atmosphere here is pretty depressing. Trading is already very slow, and the future looks gloomy ... Eugenie, Friedrich and little Marie are going for daily walks in the fresh air. We expect Emil at Easter time; from here, he will move to Wolmar. Please write a little more in detail, not only about the things around you, but I want to know what you read and how you spend the evening hours. I'd like to know the person inside you. With all the studying and work, don't become emotionally stunted. God bless you!

These letters showed us the events at the parents' house during the years 1853 and 1854 quite vividly and gave us some view into the children's families. We regret not being able to use more of Mother's letters, as space does not allow it. A few times a month, Mother used to write to Oscar to make him feel connected to the parents' house and she would talk of all the things she experienced.

Chapter 19

Friedrich's Departure from Riga, His Immigration to Germany

In April 1854, Friedrich had made up his mind to move back to Germany. On the 21st of this month, the old Vienna wagon stood fully loaded in front of the parents' house from where it was to take the travellers to Königsberg. Lina and Amalie had arrived the day before to see their siblings one more time. Actually Amalie saw her sister-in-law for the first time and then had to say goodbye forever. Theodor had driven all night to see his brother. Eugenie would have liked to stay in Riga for a few more months until her little son was stronger for this long trip on bad roads at that time of year. Mother was a bit worried. All the best wishes accompanied the travellers. "May the new country give them what they did not have here, their own property and inner peace"—these were Mother's words when they left. Nobody knew how difficult this trip was going to be. Not until May 12 did they arrive in Chemnitz, where Friedrich wanted to stay and plan the future. The trip had consisted of many adventures, which started already in Mitau. Many army transports were on the move on the road to Tauroggen, but also a heavy traffic of goods to the border had made the road in parts impassable. In Mitau, Friedrich could not get any postal horses, so he had to use some from a haulage contractor. This way, they got to Elley and stayed there for the night. The next day, he only made it to Schaulen, where he had to wait five hours for horses. Shortly after Schaulen, a wheel broke, and it took 24 hours before the trip continued. But now six horses had to be hitched because of the hilly terrain and the deep ruts left by the thousands of wagons that had used the road. Other travellers who had taken the postal coach up to this point had to take smaller wagons from Tauroggen because all heavy vehicles got stuck. Friedrich's luggage was transported by a two-horse wagon. Still he and Eugenie had to walk great parts of the way. The road past Zarizyn led through mostly swampland. The wheels of the many vehicles had cut the top stone layers, and it was dangerous to negotiate, made worse at the places where repairs had been done to put logs and branches on the soft sand. These spots had to be carefully avoided by the driver. They took the train then from Königsberg on, and all difficulties were behind them. Our travellers had traversed the road from Riga to the border with luck and without getting hurt.

Friedrich had left with the intention of again buying an estate in Germany. He gave up this plan and became book and art dealer. He never again saw his homeland but stayed closely connected to his relatives because of the love of his parents and the affection of his siblings. They always visited their brother on their travels and enjoyed his brotherly love. This feeling was also transferred to his only son, Walter, who was born in Riga. When he was grown up, he became a doctor. To see the land of his forefathers, he and his wife travelled there to visit all the relatives for a few weeks. This short visit brought a closer connection to the land of his father, and this new interest gave him the idea to participate in the publishing of the *News about the von Boetticher Family.*

Chapter 20

Staying in Ebelshof, Summer 1854, Mother's 60th Birthday

After Friedrich had left his parents' house in April 1854, it had gotten quiet. Lina, Amalie and Theodor had left too. "I feel melancholy," wrote one of the sisters shortly after. "When I walk through the long, empty row of rooms, now occupied only by the two old folks, they don't seem too happy and deserve better. Yes, old age brings gloomy and bad times. Here is a job for someone with a young and happy nature. I think that person would get Father in a good mood again. He deserves it, because God has given us and him endless goodness and does so still."

What had brought Father's mood down was not so much loneliness but that he felt weaker and weaker and had headaches brought on by high blood pressure. This made him nervous and prevented him from doing his daily routine from which he got great satisfaction. To get him back into a happier and better state of mind, Lisinka and Minna, with their husbands, moved to Ebelshof in the summer of 1854. The old folks and Miss Müller lived alone in the big house, but it was only a few steps to the Garden House (Taube's house), where the young couples with their children had settled in.

Not only did the daughters bring entertainment, but also the men, especially the always happy and accommodating son-in-law Rodde. In the city too, things would change and bring more life into the house. Mr. Hernmarck had lived for many years in the Boetticher house and now had bought his own, so the second story where he had lived was renovated for the new inhabitants. Theodor (son-in-law) and Lisinka moved in. Lisinka's eye for a cozy interior decoration, and her skillful hands made her new apartment a very nice place. She also kept a beautiful garden. The parents lived one story up. "It is good to be able to go down a few times a day and also get short visits from Elise," so Mother wrote about her new neighborhood. Father too was happy with this arrangement.

The summer stay at Ebelshof in 1854 was shorter than usual. When the sons-in-law and their families had left for the city late in August, the parents too wished to go back. Mother's birthday was not celebrated at the farm. The parents went to Kokenhusen this time for the festivities with Carl and Theodor and also Lina and her husband. On September 7, 1854, Mother turned 60 years old. She wrote about this fest:

> We spent the day in a friendly intimate circle. It rained all day, so I went only in the morning for a walk. The Perse Valley looked beautiful with the colourful leaves, and the view down

the mountain behind the parsonage is breathtaking. Hermann is proud of his orchard and had a splendid harvest this year. The grapes at his house are ripening now, and he was happy to offer me some at my birthday.

The trip to Kokenhusen did Father good. This change of scenery made him forget his sufferings. He did the long walk to Bilsteinhof and from there to the Promeaden and back to the parsonage without rest. This awareness of his endurance lifted his mood, which changed often depending on the influences. Right to his end, it gave him great joy to help others, often giving money freely, if it was deserved.

Chapter 21

Changes in the Lives of the Two Youngest Sons

The year 1854 brought changes in the lives of the two youngest sons also. Emil's confirmation was in Wolmar in May of 1854. Mother had followed the religious instructions there through letters. Then for the confirmation, she travelled to Wolmar to be with "her youngest" on this for him so very important day. "It had been nice days," she wrote on June 1, 1854.

> In Wolmar, on Ascension Day when I was there, I had the pleasure of sitting through the last hour of instructions, which fascinated me a lot so that I wished I was able to take the complete confirmation time. Emil was very happy about the schooling there and the life at that house among his contemporaries. May his time there be blessed by God for as long as he lives! Walter's speech at the confirmation ceremony was powerful and of inner conviction and I am sure found its way into everyone's heart … On May 24th, we left Wolmar and had a few nice hours in Weidau with the Albanus … In the evening we drove to Wenden. The weather was cold and it rained, but I still walked through the

castle gardens and made the decision to look at Birkenruh the next morning. Already in Wolmar I had met the Hollander family and asked to visit them. But they had travelled to Riga to attend a funeral. Emil had asked Mr. Hollander for permission to stay with us for a few days. At night we arrived in Riga ... Today Emil went back.

Not only Mother but Emil too was disappointed not to be able to visit the Hollanders in Birkenruh. Not everything that was on the mind of the 17-year-old young man he had the courage to share with his mother. Ten years later, when his own mother was long dead, Emil spent the Witsun time in Birkenruh. There the Hollanders greeted him as their son-in-law and his new mother pressed him lovingly to her heart just like his own mother used to.

The 17-year-old had worked hard to finish his school years with excellent results. On December 20, 1854, Emil's future father-in-law wrote to his father,

Emil leaves after a short one and one half years from here with knowledge that only a few have acquired that left here to attend university. Still I wish he had spent another semester with us, but this does not mean he lacks the maturity to go to university ... I really hope he will spend all his energy to study hard so to learn to know and love the science, which will lead to higher intellectual goals without becoming vain and overbearing.

The parents gave their consent, so Emil started university in the year 1855. He left Birkenruh with his final report card. In January 1855, he wrote an exam to enter the university in Dorpat (Tartu). The parents got the positive results in the second half of January. The letters they sent to their son in Dorpat show us how happy they were.

Father wrote on January 27 and February 2, 1855:

You can imagine that I was quite a bit worried what your first letter would bring. To read that you passed the exams made me very happy. Yes, it brought tears to my eyes. I send you, my dear Emil, my innermost congratulations to the start into the university and into the world. On this day, you are a free man, but there will be danger that you may experience where only honour and your own power will protect you. I will always pray for you and hope you stay in good health. If you need more money, I promise to support you, no problem. I beg you, please, stay debt-free. For everything you need for your studies, like books and so on, things that bring you knowledge, it will be a pleasure to give you the money. And trust your father who loves you absolutely … As you know, I have a lot of problems with writing now; I wanted to finish this letter, but a visit from Carl and Adele, Lina and her daughter Minna, brother Theodor, Minna Boetticher from Mittau, they all came to Riga for my Carlsday. So this letter has to be sent and take it as it is, my dear Emil, because I cannot write any more today. Once more take my fatherly, friendly advice and always trust your loving father and please stay debt-free.

Mother had written a few days before,

The postman brought your long letter with the good news about the positive results of your exams. I am happy for you and know that you look forward to the new education. Your old father had tears in his eyes reading your letter, and this pays in a way for all the effort it took to raise the children up to this point. God keep you, my dear true Emil, on the right path, to spend your time in Dorpat in such a way to become a valuable member of society and prove you are worthy of the trust that we set in you. I hope Father and you don't mind if I send a few bottles of wine along to celebrate with friends the successful exams. For now goodbye …

These letters were printed to show the joy and affection from that time when they were written and to bring us a picture of the parents in their older days in the light of happiness.

Almost at the same time as Emil started university, Oscar felt like quitting college. For a long time, he had doubts about the subjects he took at the Klügman College. A few times, he talked to Mother, and she gave him this answer:

> Don't decide about your future yet. Check things out carefully before you start a different occupation. Speak to other people who have knowledge of the business world. Every occupation has its bad sides, the longer one works in a special field, the more interesting it gets and one tends to forget about the bad sides. Don't worry about your future and ruin your youth! Work as hard as you can! Even if you don't become a merchant, the knowledge in this field will always be helpful in the other occupations …

Perhaps his parents would not have given the okay for Oscar to leave the Klügman College so quickly, but events made that decision easy. In the summer of 1854, Oscar made a trip first into the Harz Mountains and then through the Thuringer Forest and later to see Friedrich. On this trip, he developed new eye problems, so it was necessary for him to see the eye clinic in Leipzig. There he stayed for nine weeks with pain and uncertainty about his future before he was permitted to write a few lines. As soon as his eyes got better, he developed rheumatic joint pains, which made walking difficult and very painful. Under these conditions, he was unable to go back to Lübeck (College), so he went to see Friedrich, who now lived in Dresden. Not until November did Oscar get back to Lübeck, but the long interruption of his studies and the constant eye problems made him decide to quit. Oscar was convinced he would ruin his eyesight completely if he stayed in this occupation. He took this as a message from God to switch over to become an agriculturist. The parents agreed with his decision. Oscar left Lübeck in the spring and spent time in health spas to get his health back. After that, the parents wanted him to stay in Riga over the winter and start college in the spring to study agriculture. Mother never saw her Oscar again.

Chapter 22

A Student in the Parents' House, Spoiling and Reprimanding

In the spring of 1855, Mother felt the urge once more to move to Ebelshof to enjoy the green of the meadows and the lively songs of the birds. On May 13, 1855, she wrote to Emil,

> I can hardly wait to see you here and nothing else matters. For you, life is pretty rosy, but it can be harsh; that's why we have to enjoy the good things that are offered to us. Since May 7 we have been in Ebelshof. You know how beautiful it is in the springtime. Two nightingales built their nest here and now they compete with their singing. I really hope that you can lift up Father's spirit!

The expected student from Dorpat (Tartu) did not arrive as early as the parents had hoped. In a letter Mother wrote on May 15, she says, "Enjoy your life, but make sure you have no regrets later on." He had a very extensive holiday program planned, which to execute properly, a trip to Birkenruh was first on his list. Then he travelled over land to Kokenhusen and after a few days there, via boat to Riga. Never before had Mother given him such a warm welcome as when he arrived in Ebelshof. She also liked his colourful student hat, even though in a letter to him earlier, she had asked, "To own this hat did you not spend too much time, money and effort?" She liked to see him having a good time but worried that he did not take his studies seriously enough.

"Since the few days Emil is here," she writes, "he is cheerful and had a good time at the university. The learning must be easy for him. We did not see him much here as he visits friends in the city. He is happy here and knows how to spend time wisely. One day we hosted a few students for some hours here and we enjoyed listening to their quartet singing. The young, fresh voices sounded great outside; especially good is the tenor voice of the young Wilm who needs to get more training." Further we read about Emil:

> Since June 24 he visits his siblings, attended the festivities in Eckau (50th anniversary of Probst Kuehn) and enjoys his time in Courland. Last Sunday he was with Theodor in Baldohn and next Sunday they are guests of Elise in Dubbeln; then Emil comes back to us and will stay here until the end of the holidays.

At this time, Father really spoiled his son. He enjoyed the walks with Emil and smiled when his youngest explained the world as he saw it with his youthful eyes. At the end of July, Emil went back to Dorpat. He had no way of knowing that he would never see his mother again. "Yesterday Emil left," Mother wrote to Oscar on July 28, 1855, "after celebrating for nine weeks." Since he had left the university before the semesters had ended and had left without permission from Dorpat, he now faces jail time first thing he is back." In a letter to him on August 21, 1855, she reassured him that she would have been less harsh than the Dorpat University Court and she looked at this as being of insignificance. Unlike his old father, she wrote:

> I congratulate you for getting off so easy about the Pass-story, but my wish is for you not ever to be locked up during the rest of your university days. Father thinks this could hurt you on the exam marks. This I don't believe and hope when you study hard, this misstep will be forgotten. From your letter I read that you study with great enthusiasm. May God give his rich blessings for that!

His parents did not accept everything that the Dorpat student dreamed up. In early September, the Golden Anniversary of the Kuehns in Eckau was being celebrated, and, of course, the Boetticher family was also involved in the planning of this rare occasion. Emil wanted to be part of these festivities and had asked his parents to send him the travel money. Mother answered on August 26,

I hurry to write to you … so you don't prepare for the trip already. Even though we would like to see you here at the festivities, having fun among the young people, the expense for the time and money will be too high to justify this trip. You had nine weeks, dear boy, where you had lots of fun and that's why you stay in school and if we hear that you work hard it will be a greater joy for me than having you here. About the travel money you asked for, Father and I are very surprised that you are already low in your finances. You left less than five weeks ago and the money you got for four months is already gone? Would it not have been wiser to have made your father finance minister and leave half the money with him? In tough times as now, you could have gotten the money from Mr. Töffer or whatever his name is. Now good advice is hard to come by and if you lend the money to someone, make sure to get it back. Father will not send you any funds because you promised him to spend the money carefully. If you think you know how to budget, then I advise you to send Father a short overview of your expenses so he may help you with your finances.

Since yesterday we have had real fall weather. Rain, storms, and hail change all the time and yellow leaves are falling. I hope this is over in a few days and things get friendlier ... On the last August

day, I will leave for Eckau; perhaps I can help Lina. We will think

of you; the returning grandsons will report to you about Eckau.

Goodbye, dear Emil, I hope you get over our "no" to your request.

Thinking of you with love, your Mother.

Chapter 23

Tough Times in Kokenhusen, Mother's Last Days and Her Death

Mother's trip to Eckau was cancelled. During the last days of August, news arrived from Kokenhusen that changed everything. During the time when Hermann Pacht was away for a preacher-synod in Fellin, a bad guest, dysentery, came to visit the parsonage.

Blessed with God's grace and five sons, Hermann, when he came back from the trip, found his oldest son, seven-year-old Hans, already dead. Amalie, also sick, was sitting at the bedside of another dying child; she did not have the time to write to her mother. Now, Hermann wrote in deep sorrow as he took the night watch of his beloved dead son.

Mother received the letter, and after a short period of thought, she said resolutely, "I travel." Quickly her things were packed and among them—separated—as if presentiment—all the last earthly clothing that she had long ago prepared. In the Pachts' house, she found everything terribly destroyed. The Probst (Pastor) Häusler in Ascheraden had taken two sons who had been spared in loving friendship into his house. Soon after Mother had arrived, Amalie mourned the death of a second child. The old nanny put the nine-month-old Raimund, who was also sick, in the arms of his father and said, "Sir, please hold this child. I, too, will now lie down and die." Hermann was heartbroken. Only Mother, who lived through many tough times in her life and looked deeply religiously into the future, was able to console him. September 6, she wrote from Kokenhusen:

> My dear husband, I know you long to hear all the news and so I use the day the post is shipped out to tell you the good news that Amalie's health is getting better and the Doctor spoke quite positively.

> The sorrow and grief are never ending here. Little Raimund has very bad dysentery, and since he is only nine months old and weaker than his brothers, I fear his chances of survival are minimal … We tell Amalie the little one is quite weak but not more so that she does not worry too much about her darling. May God give her strength to get over this great pain! Both children who found a loving home in Ascheraden are healthy. We are very glad that Ferdinand is okay again.

> How are you, my dear husband, and how is your health? We had a lot of rain lately, so it must have been quite cool and damp in Ebelshof. May God keep you well. If it's getting too rough, move to the city … It is nice to see the neighbors getting involved during these

hard times. Especially Mr. von Löwenstern. Today a letter arrived from the manager telling Hermann that he was ordered to offer him everything he needs in foodstuff for the sick, including wine. This is very nice and friendly of him!

I look forward to getting a letter from back home and wish that the situation here would be such that I could get back home, yet I first have to know the outcome of the little one and how well Amalie is doing before I can leave … Eight years ago today, it was Amalie's wedding day, and at that time a somewhat sober celebration because Hermann's mother had just died, but still with the hope of a long and happy life for the young couple. The past eight years brought our child great happiness but also many sorrows. Praise to God because all is coming from his Father's hand and He knows best!

A second letter that Mother had written one day later from Kokenhusen did not survive. Amalie wrote about this terrible time in the parsonage.

On September 7 (19) on the morning of her birthday, Mother went with a bouquet of flowers to Amalie's bed and put them on the table. Amalie said, "You never experienced a birthday like this in a mourning house, Mother!"

"O child," Mother replied in her serious-friendly way, "I have celebrated many birthdays with tears." Then she spoke about the birthday letter she had gotten from Father and said, "My dear man still loves me in his own way." Amalie wanted to see her little boy. Mother brought the child, who was suffering greatly, and put him in Amalie's arms, and then she bent down and kissed Amalie. "I will answer the letter of the old Father," she said. Here Amalie noticed that Mother's face was already marked by the terrible sickness. "Mommy," she said, scared, "you are ill already!"

"No, no," she answered, "it is only my old face." Then she went to her room and left Amalie with great worries.

Now she was restless and sent the nurse repeatedly to check on her mother and was told again and again, "Mrs. Council is writing."

Amalie told her husband and Dr. Schulz, whom Father had sent with the nurse right away to Kokenhusen, about her mother. They gave her the news that Mother had felt sick for a few days already but would not slow down. Now she was forced to go to bed. "It does not look too bad," Doctor Schulz remarked, "but ... the 60 years."

Amalie never saw her mother again. Mother did not suffer too much, but she got weaker all the time. She was looked after very well. Father had sent his house doctor Bornhaupt and a very good nurse to Kokenhusen, but her exhaustion got greater every day. Mother slept a lot, probably the result of the opium pills, but she had friendly, peaceful dreams. "How nice did I dream," she said often during the short waking time. "My old husband and all my lovely children surrounded me." She did not want Father to make the long trip to this house of grieving and sorrow, yet at every noise she heard, she would ask, "Did my old husband arrive?" She also asked often about the very sick little boy she had put in Amalie's arms. He would die a few hours before she did. News by courier arrived to Father daily. It was not good. The old, faithful Friederike Kuehn wanted to travel to Kokenhusen to help out, but this was not permitted. What could she have done? The news about Mother's illness had brought her son Theodor and her son-in-law Ernst Kuehn to Kokenhusen. Mother was very happy to see them. She felt that the end was coming and had the need to say loving and comforting words to all her loved ones. She spoke with intermissions and fell asleep often. For the old father, for all her children, but also for others near and far, she gave her blessings and friendly words. "May God bless your choice!" she said among other things to her son Theodor in premonition of the events that decided his future life. Only a few hours before she died did she lose consciousness. On September 14 (26), 1855, her fight was over. Two faithful Mother's eyes closed forever; a heart, rich in love, had stopped beating.

Mother's death ended a harmonious, rich and dignified life. She devoted her life to helping others, and in a self-denial service and love, she passed away. She was tired and ready to go to heaven! The noble Mother! Her family recognized her kind nature and how different she had been after she was taken from their midst. For anyone who dies like her, we should not be in sorrow, but celebrate in joyful emotion!

The coffin was brought to Riga and put into the Boetticher family crypt. Pacht had promised Mother to hold the memorial service, but shortly after her death, he got sick and was not able to leave the house. Instead her son-in-law Ernst Kuehn did the service at her graveside. They were moving words coming from the heart and going to all hearts, made to console the mourners and to give strength to the old father.

Pacht wrote to Father from Kokenhusen these loving words:

The merciful Father in heaven give you strength from above and his peace! And give you the pleasure to see poor Amalie again—soon, very soon! As soon as she is allowed, she will rush to you. May the day you put your dear wife and our Mother to her last resting place bring your broken heart heaven's rest and friendly confidence. May God help us to replace your loss as much as possible with love!

Mother did not want any splendor at her funeral. Her wish was followed. But the circle that had loved her was large, and now they stood at her quiet grave. With the exception of Friedrich and Amalie, all her children were at the funeral. Oscar, who the parents had wished would spend the winter of 1855–56 with them in Riga, had left for the trip with the hope of seeing both parents after the long separation. Emil came from Dorpat and drove to Mitau to meet his brother to tell him that Mother was gone. In a letter to Father, his daughter-in-law Eugenie showed her deep sorrow about Mother's death.

> It seems like a dream, that the dear Mother is no longer among us living. I see her clearly, as I saw her often, happy, active, helping everywhere, the dear, dear Mother. She also helped the children and me, and I thank her in her grave. Who knew that this mentally and physically strong woman would go so quickly! ... You, my dear Father, may heaven keep you strong and give you the power to get over the pain. The thought that we see each other after the troubles and fights here on earth must console us; without this hope, we would despair at the gravesides of our loved ones. May God keep you, my dear Father, to be here for your children to give them joy and faith. May he give you health and strength!

Chapter 24

Father's Isolation, Amalie's Quiet Troubles, Her Visit in Riga, Oscar's Faithful Help

The circle of children who had stood at Mother's open grave and then stayed at the parents' house for a few days was soon gone. Everyone went back to work, not without sorrow to leave their old father at this time. Only Oscar stayed home. It got lonesome and quiet in the large empty rooms of the parents' house. Even though Father liked it being peaceful, this quietness was depressing; the life and the conversations that the children had brought along were now missing. But most of all, Father wanted to see his daughter Amalie, who had suffered the most from this terrible fate. So he wrote to her on September 29, 1855:

> Eight days ago tomorrow we put the body of our dear Mother into the cold earth. I miss her everywhere. With her, you lost a lot; I lost everything! The deep pain is somewhat gone, yet the quiet sorrow is deep down in my heart, and this wound will never heal. A few times I visited Mother's grave covered with flowers and wreaths from friends and loved ones. I cried tears of the highest appreciation and sorrow for her there and thought of you and the double pain that you feel but also the providence that left you the husband and the two children.

Hurry soon to me. Here you can look after yourself better and we can comfort each other. Bring your husband and the two children along. I will send the four-seater wagon to you so you can travel in bad weather and be safe.

I know that the tough times and sickness in your house have cost money and that worries you. I would like to help you. It will be my holy duty to fulfill all of the last wishes of the blessed Mother; all I ask is that my children come openly with their requests to me … I send to you … rubles. The small coach, that was Mother's, is now yours, dear Amalie … It has a sled undercarriage and will serve you in winter and summer. Keep the doctor and nurse as long as you need them and tell them to ask me for their reimbursements. As soon as the carriage arrives please hurry into the arms of your eagerly waiting, sad, faithful and loving Father.

Father's dear wish did not become reality soon. The joyful sounds of the happy children that had filled the house in Kokenhusen were now gone, and the worries would not leave. Amalie had cried bitterly about the death of her three sons, but she did not complain. Now that Mother was sick, she got gloomy and her heart heavy, and she had to think often how much not only she had lost with her but also Father and her siblings. Her thoughts were always with her old father who had lost the love and care of Mother and now waited impatiently for her to be ready for the trip. The terrible sickness had taken its toll; her weak legs hardly carried her, and her shaking hands were useless for any work. And she still worried about her husband, the doctors saying he was fine at the moment but that could change quickly. Weeks passed before Hermann Pacht was fine and Amalie had enough strength to make the trip to Riga in short day intervals. The presence of both in Riga but especially Amalie's managing the household, which reminded Father of his wife and her love towards him, all helped a lot to ease the pain. The daughters and sons-in-law living in Riga also provided love and support, but most of all, Oscar was there to help Father. During the six months after Mother's death, he lived at his parents' house and became Father's secretary and business manager. All his siblings living further away came to him with different questions concerning business ventures. He helped them and wrote the letters for Father, who had problems with writing. Oscar's friendly nature and the patience he had learned early on in his life during the time of his sufferings made him the perfect candidate to help Father faithfully. He in return recognized his loving help, and Father's mood improved greatly.

Chapter 25

New Joy and New Sorrow, Theodor's Engagement and Ernst Kuehn's Death, Theodor's Wedding, Lina Moves to Father's

There were often visitors from the country, but most often Theodor showed up in Riga. He was not able to hide what was on his mind for a long time. He wanted to make Father happy with his visits, but there was something else that brought him from his quiet Arzen often to Riga. Before the year 1855 with its sorrowful memories was over, Mother's prediction before her death became reality. Theodor introduced the new daughter to Father, the one Mother had given her blessings to, and now he was the happy husband-to-be of Alexandra von Sengbusch. Nobody was more joyful for this connection than the old father. The lovely bride brought all the good characteristics for the one who had won her heart. With her charm, her warm heart, and her intellect, she quickly won over the large family circle that Theodor introduced her to, and during the years afterwards, their love and admiration for her grew steadily. Mother's passing and the loss of Amalie's children had shocked the house deeply, but Theodor's engagement brought new joy. Father forgot the physical pains that bothered him, and at year's end, the wish, after the many unhappy memories, for everyone was to have a better year, less pain for Father and a long life for him among his children and grandchildren. Indeed, this wish seemed to be coming true.

But then the family experienced another heavy blow. After a short illness, Ernst Kuehn died on January 22 (February 3), 1856—he who had conducted Mother's funeral services a few months before and had given uplifting words to all the ones grieving. Who knew that this strong man full of life would die so young? He was in his best years and could have served his large family and congregation for many more years. God thought differently. It was said, "We don't know any other form of evolution, as the one presented to us on our star. What is this span of time to the eternity of the spirit?" *Evolution* was the word most often used of dear Ernst. How beautifully did he evolve!

After her husband had passed away, Lina stayed another one and a half years in Eckau. It was a heavy blow for her. The house where she had spent the happiest times of her life at the side of Ernst's great personality had now lost its appeal. The weak health she was in made her position especially difficult after the year of mourning for the widow of a pastor. Yet it was not easy for her to leave Eckau, even though Father pleaded with her to move with all her children to him.

For the last year, Father had felt lonely. A friendly old lady, Mrs. Kueker, managed the household for him. With her undemanding nature, she looked after him lovingly, always there to help the relatives living in the countryside for whom the parents, for a long time, felt responsible. Emil, the youngest son, who had spent some of his holidays with Father, got to know Mrs. Kueker and appreciated her a lot. Oscar had stayed healthy during the rough winter months in Riga and left Father in the summer of 1856 to study agriculture at a university in Germany. Before he left, he attended a family ceremony that Mother too would have liked to see happening, even though the year of mourning had not passed yet. Theodor got married on June 14 (26), 1856, and Oscar and Emil led the couple as marshals to the altar. Superintendent Poelchau in the Martin Church conducted the ceremony, and the festivities were at the von Sengbusch Villa Schönhof. A few weeks later, Theodor and his young bride moved first to Arzen, and later on, they moved close by into the newly bought Mariaculm. When Oscar left, Father lost his steady companion, and after the summer holidays were over and Emil had left for Dorpat too, he felt lonely. During the year 1856, his health had improved so at Christmastime he decided to make a round trip to visit his children living in Courland. This gave him renewed energy; seeing his sons' farming activities brought him special happiness. On the other side, Lina's health worried him, and her position in the parsonage in Eckau was not to his liking. Father still wanted her and the children to move into his house. But Lina was reluctant to leave since her father-in-law had health problems. After his son's death, the old probst had taken over the preacher position in Eckau again with the help of a vicar. The year of mourning was now over for Lina, and Father still pushed her to move in with him. So first off, she was to leave her place and to boost her health stay in a spa close to the sea. To make his point, Father wrote to her on June 21, 1857:

> I am sorry to read in your letter that your father-in-law is not well. Emil said the same. You want to look after him and take care. A nice and noble thought, it is the duty of a child! But whoever wants to do this has to be strong and healthy first of all, especially if one has the means and time to do so. You have both, but not the power to stop the change of seasons ... My doctor was the first one who pointed out to me that only peace and quiet and a spa treatment would restore your strength; and this I want to discuss with you. You are a religious woman, but it is sinful of you not to look after your health. Think about my proposal. If you and your children go to a sea spa to recuperate, you will give the loving children and faithful relatives who all want to look after the health of the probst and his wife, a chance to do so. Your position will be replaced. You have the time, and the money comes from me ... Lisinka and Minna are already at the beach, so go

and recuperate there! Those of your children who don't need the spa treatment can stay at Ebelshof to make it easier for you. My love for you makes my old heart heavy, especially since my body gets weaker every day too and things could be different … So take my advice and tell me the day that I can send someone to pick you and all your children up. Do not increase the sorrows of a widower's life. But at least think of the money that I feel is my sense of duty as love to you well spent. I cannot write and say much. What I have said to you in this letter is a guaranty, so keep it as a document … God keep you for all of us, but especially for your children. May he give your parents-in-law the best of health! Your faithful Father.

The letter had the desired effect. Lina moved to the beaches first (Summer 1856), and then in August, she closed down her household in Eckau and moved with her children to Father's. For him, this was a new beginning.

He was quite excited and helped to make this move for his daughter as easy as possible. He got up at five o'clock in the morning to inspect the wagons that left Ebelshof on August 6 to pick up Lina's things in Eckau. He hoped for good weather because rain could make the transport difficult. A carpenter and his tools went along to look after the wooden crates; he sent straw and mats also as packing material and sweets for the grandchildren on their trip to Ebelshof. In the letter he sent along, it says, "If the customs control near Riga (where they inspect the travellers for liquor) wants to search the wagons, so let them send a person along to Ebelshof and examine the luggage here."

Lina was again in Father's house. She cared for him, and the cheerful children brought new life into the empty rooms. He was not alone anymore, and he enjoyed the grandchildren and was happy that Lina was near. But his vitality had been gone since the death of his faithful partner, who with all his undertakings maybe without realizing it had helped make his decisions. He was tired now and longed for the hour when God would call him. His memory was bad, and often he looked for things and paused a moment to think of what he was looking for. If someone offered to help him, he replied in a friendly but almost scared way, "No, no, you will probably even misplace more things." He was very orderly and never went to bed at night before everything was neat and tidy as if it were his last hour. His memory loss weighed heavy on him. It can't be said that he had found a new meaning in life after Lina's move even though at times the happy activities of the young generation made him cheerful.

Chapter 26

A Sad Christmas, Losses for Lina and Elise, Eugenie's Death

These happy activities would end soon. Among the grandchildren, measles and then shortly diphtheria had broken out. In November 1857, the youngest of the children died, and four weeks later, another one died. Others were sick too, and the worries lasted right through Christmastime. In vain were the efforts to keep these contagious diseases away from the lower level where Lisinka with her family lived. Besides her stepson, Gustav, Lisinka had her own child, Philipp, born November 27, 1852. He was small with a frail constitution. Little Philipp got sick and passed away on December 27 (January 8), 1857–58. This sacrifice was not enough; death took Lina's six-year-old Mathilde in January 1858.

It was a very bad time, and the old grandfather felt the pain that cut into the mother's heart also. These sad experiences linger for a long time, and it takes even longer for happiness to move back. Everybody was still mourning when news arrived from Dresden that Friedrich's wife, Eugenie, had died on June 2, 1858. She did not recuperate after giving birth to her youngest child. Death took her away from her four children, the youngest only eight days old.

Chapter 27

Elise's Trip and Lina Staying at the Beaches, Father's Thoughtful Caring, Theodor in Ebelshof

The old father had known many tough times and got through all these in his own loving way. Helping others gave him great satisfaction, and this in turn directed his life. He had lived with Lina's and Lisinka's pain and saw the grief in their faces. He also knew that Lina's health was not good after the time of hardship. Now he made sure his daughters got time off to recuperate. Not thinking that he would be lonely, he sent Lisinka, her husband, and her stepson in the springtime on a trip into a foreign country and Lina and her family to Peterskapelle at the beaches.

He himself moved for the summer again to Ebelshof, where he put the management into the hands of Theodor, who in the meantime had sold his Estate Arzen and now from Ebelshof was looking for a new farm.

Father had some regrets after he had given the management of his special place, Ebelshof, to his son. To relinquish this control over Ebelshof was harder for him than the separation from his daughters and grandchildren, who had left him during the summer of 1858.

He was very much interested in Lina's well-being during her stay in Peterskapelle, which we see from a letter to her.

Ebelshof, July 4, 1858

A few ... days ago you left for the beaches and only now did I get news from you. I welcome you in Peterskapelle, and I'm happy to hear that you are all in good health and spirit, even though with an empty stomach. Because hunger and thirst cannot be satisfied as you write with little indigestible stones and water from the sea. And catching the fish that are also in it will be a tough job for Peter and Leo. Perhaps Walter (Pacht) can help with this ... I told the compassioned Hintersdorff to supply you, my dear children, with foodstuff so you don't go hungry. Your beach is known for this ... If you ask me, I would love to pay for everything, so my dear children don't lack anything, just let me know before what you need ... May you, Amalie and the children recuperate well at the beach ...

Yesterday I got news from Friedrich. The body is okay, but his heart and spirit have suffered like any man who has lost his loving wife, his half; where the mother of the children, the faithful wife, the advisor and housewife is missing, everything is gone. Friedrich's mother-in-law moves to her ailing daughter Stoeckardt. An older widow, an educated lady from Erfurt, looks after his children. The youngest is seven weeks old now and very cute; she gets a nurse. The loving father Friedrich is not giving any of his children away, even though Lisinka gave him gentle advice …

Chapter 28

Oscar at the University and His Visit in Riga, Emil Back Home, His Trips to Foreign Countries, One of Father's Last Letters

In late summer of 1858, Oscar with Lisinka and her husband came back to Riga. On his way to study agriculture in Germany in summer 1856, he had to make a stopover in Berlin. There an eye infection needed to be looked after at the von Graefe Clinic. Only many months later was he able to continue his trip after the successful operation. He went to Dresden first and stayed until the fall of 1856 and the start of the university semester. At the university in Poppelsdorf-Bonn, he began his studies in his chosen field and really enjoyed the student life, the one that had evaded him because of his illness. He made trips during the school holidays and wrote about them and his stay in Bonn to Father, who greatly enjoyed them. Oscar was back in 1858, but for a short time only. He left in the fall to start his practical training in Germany. To see his son, who during the time of the illness had worried him a lot, now in good shape and happy, brought him joy. At the end of the year 1858, Emil made his candidate exam, and in February 1859, he got the candidate diploma from the university in Dorpat. This too made Father very happy. Now he would have liked

Emil back in Riga. He was to occupy the upper story of his house and to look for a job as a public servant. Father would do anything to help him establish his own household. If Emil could have known that Father had only a short time to live, he would not have left him. Now he felt this great pull to see God's beautiful world, the one he had read and heard a lot about and had some memories about from the time of his early youth. Many of the children showed up from the country to celebrate Father's 77th birthday. A few days later, Emil left for Germany, first to recuperate from the strain of the last year studying at the university and then to continue his education at German institutions.

Most often, the news that Father received was good. His life went in a quiet way, without major events to upset his mind; only his body lost its strength. Sitting on the couch, he often fell asleep while people were talking or if someone read the paper to him. He kept himself busy all the time; even though he had given up his bookkeeping, he still wrote all his letters, which were quite numerous, with a steady hand.

In a letter from Father to Amalie on August 10, 1859, we find the same good penmanship that he had been known for 50 years earlier. The content of this letter is also of interest, so here it is:

I hope that you and all your children are well and that you think often about a trip where I expect you and your children soon. I informed Hermann about it too. He and his Father are well. Through the arrangement of Friedrich in Dresden I sent money, but I probably have to send more. Hermann, who thinks you are in Riga, told me to send a sum of money to you. This money and more, if you need it, are here for you, but during the last two weeks I found no way of getting it to you so you would have at least some for the trip. This old man would have liked to surprise you with a visit in Kokenhusen, but I did not have the energy. Adele is here since yesterday; she just wanted to see me again.

Writing is getting tougher now, even though I have to write a lot, so I hope to see you here soon.

I hope you haven't forgotten about me—and if you're here we will talk about all the things that I was not able to write. Now goodbye and think often with love of your old Father.

Father wrote this letter four weeks before he died at a time when he knew his end was near and he felt the inexpressible longing to see his dear Amalie one more time. With all the signs of weakness that come through in this letter, Father reveals an obviously strong desire to finish all the business that he had at hand. And how friendly did he think of his son-in-law Pacht, who was on a trip and needed money at that time. This was also the case with Amalie, so she was able to visit him!

Chapter 29

Father's Last Hours and His Death

After Amalie had visited Father, she left for home and he left extraordinarily early from Ebelshof to go back to the city. Mother's birthday was coming up, and obviously on this day that had previously been so much celebrated at Ebelshof, he did not want to be there.

On the evening before September 6 (18), he felt very sick. In his considerate way, he did not tolerate Lina staying up for him, but after she had pleaded with him, he allowed the butler to sleep in the hall next to his room. He was very restless now. He organized his papers, and very late, he lay down half-dressed. The butler had asked him repeatedly, "Should I call your daughter? Should I call for the doctor?"

"No" was the answer. "Don't you bother anybody." But the old father could not sleep.

At six o'clock in the morning on September 6, Lina went to his bedside. She found him very sick and immediately sent for Dr. Bornhaupt. Soon his daughter Lisinka with her husband, Theodor, stood by his side. His faithful coachman Hans Weide went quickly to Rodde to bring the news with trembling lips: "Our old councillor is very sick." When the adopted daughter Minna and her husband arrived, she found her old father on his bed in the middle of the room. There he was, lying half-dressed, the little black cap on his head, a silk scarf around his neck, the hands folded on his chest, a blessed, already blissful smile on his friendly face—a picture of blessed peace. He opened his eyes, looked in a friendly way at Minna and Rodde and stroked the hands of both.

He seldom talked now. The news of his sickness had spread quickly. Many came to see him once more. All the people came from Ebelshof to the city to see the old gentleman. "Let all my dear people come," he had said. And as the mourners stood around his deathbed, he turned to them with the words "I thank you. I thank all of you." He had words of thanks for all his loved ones. He obviously had no pain. He rested quietly and peacefully. A few times, he asked, "Is it seven o'clock soon?" And as the clock had sounded seven times, he had softly passed away. Two days before when he heard the news that a man in his best years had died, he said, "God has called this young, strong man who could have been of good use to many thousands, and me the poor old man, he does not take!" Now his wish was fulfilled; God's mercy had softly and blissfully relieved him.

His life and work had been richly blessed, but the peace that his soul desired, he did not find in this world. His energy was broken when his faithful partner had been ripped from his side.

Chapter 30

At the Grave

Mother had wished for Herman Pacht to officiate at her graveside, but he was unable to do so. Now he followed up this wish at Father's grave. His text: "Blessed be the ones that suffer, because they will be comforted."

The speaker used these Bible words to remind the bereaved not to shy away from suffering but to strive to improve the inner person towards love. This alone would lead to helping each other and would create comfort, joy and peace for everyone.

About the Author

Jürgen von Boetticher was born in Germany on January 1, 1937, in Steinau, Silesia, and emigrated to Canada in 1962. He is a master craftsman in the automotive repair trade. He owned numerous new car dealerships before retiring in 1990. He is an avid reader of books about European history and has translated several books about the von Boetticher family. Jürgen has two children and three grandchildren and lives on his hobby farm near Durham, Ontario.

Printed in the United States
By Bookmasters